ROBERTS LIARDON

HOW TO
Flow
IN THE TIMINGS
OF
God

EMBASSY
PUBLISHING

How To Flow in the Timings of God:
 Keys To Unlocking God's Power and Fulfilling His Plan

Roberts Liardon Ministries
P. O. Box 4215
Sarasota, FL 34230

E-mail: info@robertsliardon.org
www.RobertsLiardon.org

ISBN 978-17336062-5-7
eBook ISBN 978-1-7336062-6-4

Formerly *The Price of Spiritual Power,* copyright 1989.

New Edition © 2022 by Roberts Liardon

Editorial Consultant: Cynthia D. Hansen
Text Design: Lisa Simpson, www.SimpsonProductions.net

Contents

Preface

Jesus never moved out of God's timing and season for Him, nor did He veer from the prophecies written in the Word concerning Him. Jesus never allowed other people to move Him off course or out of sync with the Spirit.

Some wanted to make Jesus king, but He resisted them and went to the Cross. He lived to please His Father, which ultimately resulted in the greatest blessing to all people.

And Jesus is our Example.

God chose us to be born into the generation that would live at the very end of the Church Age. That means He has given us everything we need to navigate the turbulence of this transitional season called the last of the last days.

Now it's up to us to take advantage of what He's provided for us. It's up to us to pursue Him with a hunger that can never be satisfied — to become experts at hearing the voice of His Spirit and flowing with His timings as we fulfill His good plan for our lives.

I need to warn you — this pursuit doesn't always come easy. There is a price to pay to intimately know and to seamlessly flow with the Lord. *But, oh, the reward* when Jesus looks in your eyes on that day and says, "Well done, good and faithful servant."

Imagine experiencing that moment — a deep assurance that your Savior is pleased with you as you come to the end of your spiritual race. Nothing compares with the wealth and the worth of that reward. And nothing is more important than learning and applying the truths that will ensure that this will be *your* outcome one day.

Roberts Liardon
Sarasota, Florida
Spring 2022

Yet indeed I also count all things loss
for the excellence of the knowledge of Christ Jesus my Lord,
for whom I have suffered the loss of all things,
and count them as rubbish, that I may gain Christ.
— Philippians 3:13 NKJV

Introduction

You have a call on your life to fulfill a certain purpose — your part in God's plan — while you're on this earth. And whatever is included in that divine assignment, I can guarantee you this: It will require you to know His voice, discern His timings, and access His power if you are going to fulfill your call the way He intends for you to do it.

So before you even turn the next page to read what God wants to say to you about paying the price to flow in His timings and fully accomplish His will, I want to speak to that gift in you, placed there by God Himself.

⭐ I command your gift to begin to come alive in a fresh way — to be stirred and to come forth and make itself known to you and to the earth.

⭐ I command every wrong voice to be removed out of your life and the right voice of instruction and encouragement to take its place.

⭐ I break the power of illegal utterances and false prophecies spoken over your life, and I command them to die and to stop directing your thoughts, your feelings, and your behaviors. I declare that the Scriptures and the true prophetic words spoken over you will come alive to you and function as the burning motivation of your heart and life.

If you have made mistakes in the past, if you've grown cold in your soul, or if you have been a hearer only and not a doer of the Word, I ask you to take the time now, before you continue reading this book, to identify your sin and repent of it.

Ask God to forgive you. Ask Him to use you for His glory every day of your life from this day forward. He's a Forgiver and a Restorer. You've never done anything that made God regret that He called you or gifted you the way that He has or that caused Him to take His gifts and calling away from you (*see* Rom. 11:29).

I bind every spirit of the enemy that has put you in some type of captivity in the Name of Jesus. May the growth of your spirit and your gift come alive again even as you read the pages that follow. I loose you from being confined to the box of man's religious expectations. I declare that the contents of this book will help release you into your appointed domain in this world and into your call and destiny.

If you are grieving over all the time that you have wasted in life, remember that God can redeem the time you've lost, so don't give up and don't think it's over. Let the words of this book help stir you up to a new level of momentum in your pursuit of Jesus and the power of His Spirit as you learn to flow in *His* timings. God can pack more into five years than what you've done in the past 50 if you'll ask Him and be willing just to roll with Him! It's not over until you leave this world!

The call of God on your life, no matter what it is, abides with you forever. The Holy Spirit will help you discover your gifts and your talents so you can bring your supply into the earth and the world can be lifted by it.

That's what we're after in this book — God's gifts and calling in your life, produced according to the "when" and the "how" of His plan for you. There is no other way to do it! To fulfill what God has called you to do, you must hunger for more of Him and for His touch of mighty power.

So open your heart, your mind, and your life to God as you read the following pages. Just yield yourself to the Holy Spirit and allow Him to work in you what is needed. He wants to use you as a conduit of His spiritual power — for His glory and for His love of humanity.

Be forewarned again: There's a price to pay for it. There is a hunger required to obtain it. And there is a way to go about it — in *His* way, in *His* time. But, oh, there is a mighty reward for obeying from your heart all He is asking you to do, for pressing in day by day to receive more of Him. I can tell you from personal experience that *nothing* can compare to the supernatural adventure of living continually in God's presence and learning to let His power continually flow through you to accomplish what He has called you to do!

Part 1

RIGHT
SPIRITUAL TIMING

CHAPTER 1

⭐ Time Can Be Your Friend ⭐

That he no longer should live the rest of his time in the flesh to the lusts of men, but to the will of God.

1 Peter 4:2

As the Body of Christ, we need to understand that God has a perspective from which every arena of our lives operates, whether individually or corporately. That perspective is called "time." The choice of how to operate in line with that one word "time" determines whether people's lives move forward in God or stumble backward and whether nations are able to advance spiritually or regress. It all depends on *understanding* and *cooperating* with the timing of God.

One of the greatest needs we have as Christians involves understanding and operating within God's spiritual timing. As soon as we are born again, the sensitivity to the timing of

God should operate in our lives. Every moment from that point forward is meant to be lived according to the will of the Father.

The world has made an attempt to harness time. People have created time-management seminars and have tried to teach millions how to save time and use it more effectively. I am not against time management by any means, but some have become so "time consumed" that they have allowed their values to deteriorate — as long as it saves some time.

**The choice of how to operate in line
with that one word "time"
determines whether people's lives
move forward in God or stumble backward
and whether nations are able
to advance spiritually or regress.**

Earth time usually means "rush." We have fast-food restaurants, rush-hour traffic, instant this and instant that. People in the natural fight with time; it frustrates them and produces anger. They don't like the pace of it. They either want time to slow down or to speed up.

FINE-TUNING TO GOD'S TIME

To the world, time is an enemy, but time becomes the friend of those who live in touch with the Spirit realm. People who live in the Spirit know how to work and walk with time.

God introduced His timing to us from the very first: "In the beginning God created the heaven and the earth" (Gen. 1:1).

That first verse in the Bible introduces us to God's timing. Everything He did that was recorded in Scripture was based on timing. When He created the universe, He made each part of it on a certain day at a certain time. He formed every part of the galaxy to operate in His timing. First, He created the earth and everything surrounding it. Then God created all the plants, fish, animals, and birds. Finally, in His perfect timing, He created man. At this point, all of God's creation walked harmoniously with Him.

Time becomes the friend of those who live in touch with the Spirit realm. People who live in the Spirit know how to work and walk with time.

But in Genesis 3, when Adam and Eve sinned and ate of the forbidden fruit, they fell from the grace of God and began operating out of their own timing. They lost their ability to hear and follow God without a special endowment from Heaven. They no longer had the ability to operate in God's timing on their own. Every generation since then has seen only trials and troubles unless God has intervened.

All through Old Testament days, God gave information to the people concerning Himself through the prophets. He still provided them with the ability to know and serve Him. The understanding of spiritual times, even in those days, came as a result of a life committed to God.

One of the things Jesus came and produced for us at Calvary was the ability to perceive and regain the correct timing of God. By receiving Jesus' redemption and walking in the Spirit, we can fine-tune our spirits to know when to be in the right place at the right time. God builds His character within us so that our decisions can line up with His will — decisions that will position us strategically in the proper season.

When a person lives in the Spirit, time is a blessing. Spirit-filled people can walk in step with God and work the works of God without stress or strain. They understand God's timing and, as a result, they understand that timing is on their side. Time means stability and nurturing. Time matures and heals. It brings understanding and strengthened abilities.

By receiving Jesus' redemption and walking in the Spirit, we can fine-tune our spirits to know when to be in the right place at the right time.

Time expands and deepens our insight. When we understand God's timing, we walk with patience. As a result, we have the ability to possess our whole man — physically, emotionally, and spiritually.

Walking securely in the timings of God alleviates all fear and doubt. Godly timing produces courage, boldness, security, and strength.

God's clock is always ticking but doesn't resemble the human clock. If we follow the human clock, many would say we're about to run out of time. But we who truly know God can rest in the understanding of His ways and His timing.

Life in the Spirit realm has a timing to it just as life in the natural realm does. If you stay close to the Lord, you will be able to move according to His seasons to fulfill His plan for your life.

We must learn that it's not always right to move into action just because it seems like the right thing to do. It is important for us to follow the Holy Spirit's leading. This kind of obedience is only possible by spending much time alone with God in prayer and intercession.

Prayer alerts your spirit to the commands of Heaven. It causes your spirit man to take precedence over your mind, resulting in the right action at the right time.

If you will walk strongly in the Spirit, you will be able to move according to God's clock in everything you do. You will know how much time to spend with certain people, when to build relationships, when to speak, and when to withhold. You will know when to move out on the plan of God for your family, your church, your community, and your nation.

We must learn that it's not always right to move into action just because it seems like the right thing to do. It is important for us to follow the Holy Spirit's leading.

You never have to miss the correct timing of God in your life. Jesus is your Example. He knew when the time had come to fulfill the greatest work ever to be done — the redemption for all mankind at Calvary.

> **Then He [Jesus] came the third time and said to them, "Are you still sleeping and resting? It is enough! The hour has come; behold, the Son of Man is being betrayed into the hands of sinners. Rise, let us be going. See, My betrayer is at hand."**
>
> **Mark 14:41-42 NKJV**

Some people miss the accurate time to enter the ministry. They know that God has called them, but their time hasn't yet come because there is a need for a time of preparation. Sadly, many have launched out too soon and aborted their entire ministry because they gave God no time to properly equip them to handle the trouble they would encounter.

> **...A wise man's heart discerns both time and judgment.**
>
> **Ecclesiastes 8:5 NKJV**

We must be able to know when to go and when to stay, when to speak and when to remain silent. It is my goal to accurately hit the timing of God every time so Heaven can reap the benefit of a full and bountiful harvest through my life.

It is the will of God that we not only be sensitive to the leadings of the Holy Spirit, but that we operate effectively in them. Time is designed by God to be one of our dearest friends.

CHAPTER

Discerning Times and Seasons

Then He [Jesus] also said to the multitudes, "Whenever you see a cloud rising out of the west, immediately you say, 'A shower is coming'; and so it is. And when you see the south wind blow, you say, 'There will be hot weather'; and there is. Hypocrites! You can discern the face of the sky and of the earth, but how is it you do not discern this time?"

Luke 12:54-56 NKJV

If we didn't understand natural times and seasons, we might go out in the dead of winter in T-shirts and shorts and freeze to death. On the other hand, we might go outside in the tropics during the summer wearing overcoats and thermal underwear and have heatstroke!

Jesus addressed this spiritual principle while teaching His disciples, the ever-present Pharisees, and "an innumerable multitude of people" on this particular day in Galilee (*see* Luke 12:1 NKJV). Jesus was fervent in His illustration and didn't give His listeners any excuse for ignorance. In fact, He called them hypocrites. That was a very bold statement!

Jesus' implication was that His hearers should have known from Old Testament Scripture that they were living in the time of the Messiah. He didn't confine His remarks, as He sometimes did, just to His disciples or to a portion of the crowd. This time He chastised the entire multitude of people listening to Him!

I believe that if Jesus were walking on the earth today and the Church could see Him with natural eyes, He would be saying something similar to every believer. Jesus not only desires but *expects* the faithful to discern spiritual times.

We live in a new day, a new spiritual time. When Jesus said, "...Let the dead bury their own dead..." (Luke 9:60 NKJV), He meant, "Let the past be the past." You cannot make spiritual progress if you never look beyond past moves of God, any more than you can have growth in your natural life while living in the past.

**Jesus not only desires but *expects* the faithful
to discern spiritual times.**

Jesus said to the multitudes that day in Galilee, "How is it that you know all about the natural side of life, but you cannot tell what times you are in on the spiritual side?" God does not live in the past. It is always *today* with the Lord. He lives in the now. The greatest results you will have in your life and ministry will come when you walk in the spiritual time in which you are living — when you walk in God's *present* anointing.

We are to learn from the past, but we are not to live there. We are to live in the present and look to the future. We must learn to think in the now, or we will not see God's glory as we should, nor will we be able to move with Him when He moves.

Many churches cherish a time in the past so much that they build a memorial to it in their minds and live there. But the best way to respect the past is to build on it for the future.

The great men and women of the Church's past would be the first to push us on out to forge forward on the path they laid. They're cheering us on to move forward and to take God's plan further! They wouldn't be happy to learn that the Church is living on past glories of what He accomplished through them in an earlier time.

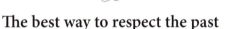

**The best way to respect the past
is to build on it for the future.**

Of course, we need to honor past men and women of God. We need to appreciate and learn from what they accomplished for God's Kingdom. But we can only live, move, and have our being *in God*, not in what past generations accomplished. The past reputation of the Church, no matter how great, is not the rock on which we are to stand. To receive today's blessing, we must move in what God is doing today.

It is not the season to act like we are about to leave the earth. It is the season to hear from Heaven so we can reap the harvest — the full potential of souls in all the earth. It is the season to declare the works of God in the nations. It is time to regain our sensitivity to repentance!

The trumpet has not yet sounded, and we are not in the season to put on the wedding gown. We are betrothed, but we are still wearing army clothes. Wearing a wedding gown in a season of war and harvest would make us stand out as an easy target for the enemy.

We must set ourselves to hear accurately what the Spirit of the Lord is doing in the earth today. If Jesus comes back tomorrow, we need Him to find us fulfilling our appointed part in the work of the ministry, not sitting around waiting for something to happen.

The subject of warfare should not make you nervous. Those who do not understand the season of transition get very touchy about spiritual warfare. They don't understand that a time of transition, a day of visitation from the Lord, always means spiritual warfare. Hard work always comes before the harvest.

**We must set ourselves to hear accurately what
the Spirit of the Lord is doing in the earth today.**

In Jesus' day, Satan himself came to war against the Messiah. It was a time of transition. Demons were stirred up everywhere Jesus went. He cast them out and taught His disciples to cast them out. Then Jesus made deliverance part of the Great

Commission — His final instructions of war to His "soldiers" (*see* Mark 16:15-18).

The time of preparation for God's move has been going on for several years now; revival is in progress worldwide. But God intends revival for *the Church*, not for sinners. Revival means "restoration," and something cannot be restored that has never been. The Body of Christ always needs refreshing and restoration before great moves of evangelism and harvest. God uses those times to prepare the "soil" in the hearts of His people before He gathers in the lost.

Revival must not be confused with *evangelism.* God revives local churches; then they go out and evangelize, gathering in the harvest. Evangelism is the offspring of a church whose heart has been revived.

If people are living in the past while hearing the message for today, the message won't make any sense to them. They may think it is false or confusing, and they will probably want to come against it — just as the Pharisees did in Jesus' day.

The Pharisees were trying to live in the past glory of Israel. They had built a memorial to Moses and the Law and were looking backward instead of forward to the New Covenant whose time had come.

You can choose to live in any time zone you want to live as a Christian. You have the choice to live in the past, if you so desire. You have the opportunity to sit and wait for the coming of the Lord. But to live on the cutting edge and to be fully alive with the Spirit of God is to move with what He is doing in the earth right now — *today.*

The Pharisees didn't hear Heaven's message that was being proclaimed in their day. Although they were to lead the people, they didn't know the season and timing of God.

To live on the cutting edge and to be fully alive with the Spirit of God is to move with what He is doing in the earth right now — *today*.

However, the demons knew the spiritual time. When Jesus cast a legion of demons out of the two demon-possessed men, the evil spirits spoke to Him of that time: "And, behold, they cried out, saying, What have we to do with thee, Jesus, thou Son of God? art thou come hither to torment us before the time?" (Matt. 8:29).

You see, even demons are aware that God has set times to do certain things. They knew it was not His time for them to be shut up forever in the lake of fire.

Demons who operate in the low, carnal area are not very intelligent. They don't think or reason. However, those workers for Satan who are part of his hierarchy — the principalities, powers, and rulers of darkness (*see* Eph. 6:12) — know what God has said in His Word about set times. If the devil and his demons know of God's timings, certainly His people should set themselves to know.

JOHN THE BAPTIST'S EXAMPLE
DURING THE GREAT TRANSITION

The three years that covered the ministry of John the Baptist and Jesus were a time of major transition from the Old Covenant to the New Covenant. That is why Jesus' first and only message in His hometown of Nazareth made a clear statement regarding the spiritual season they were in.

> **And he came to Nazareth, where he had been brought up: and, as his custom was, he went into the synagogue on the sabbath day, and stood up for to read.**
>
> **Luke 4:16**

Jesus was accustomed to going into the synagogue and reading the text for the day. The people knew Him. This was not the first time He had read from the Scriptures. Verse 17 says that they gave Jesus the book of Isaiah to read.

God had appointed this very day for Jesus to declare to His family and neighbors who He was. In God's time, Jesus read from the prophetic book of Isaiah. Because the people of Nazareth had known Jesus all of His life, they got the first opportunity to hear that the day of visitation was at hand.

Many times when God sends someone out on an assignment, He sends that person first to his or her family and friends.

Jesus, sensitive in His spirit, followed God's timing, although He must have known it would make the religious crowd angry. We must follow Jesus' example today. God arranges situations in His timing, and it is important that we don't get in His way.

> **The Spirit of the Lord is upon me, because he hath anointed me to preach the gospel to the poor; he hath sent me to heal the brokenhearted, to preach deliverance to the captives, and recovering of sight to the blind, to set at liberty them that are bruised, to preach the acceptable year of the Lord.... And he began to say unto them, This day is this scripture fulfilled in your ears.**
>
> **Luke 4:18-19,21**

"The acceptable year of the Lord" explicitly states the time on God's clock. Those words prophesied the coming Messiah, and those who were present knew it. But the listeners missed their day of visitation because they clung to a past time of God. They had grown comfortable in the past that they understood.

Jesus tried to tell the people who were present in the synagogue that day, "These things were foretold for a certain day. Now that day has arrived. It is *today*." But they would not hear. They could not sense the appointed time and season of God.

> The listeners missed their day of visitation
> because they clung to a past time of God.
> They had grown comfortable
> in the past that they understood.

John the Baptist also proclaimed the timing of God in that day.

> **And saying, Repent ye: for the kingdom of heaven is at hand.... I indeed baptize you with water unto repentance: but he that cometh after me is mightier than I, whose shoes I am not worthy to bear: he shall baptize you with the Holy Ghost, and with fire.**
>
> **Matthew 3:2,11**

Then the very next day, John saw Jesus and said:

> **This is he of whom I said, After me cometh a man which is preferred before me: for he was before me.**
>
> **John 1:30**

After John baptized Jesus and the Holy Spirit descended on Him in the form of a dove, John knew that Jesus was the Son of God. God had given that sign to acknowledge who Jesus is (*see* John 1:31-34).

John knew that he had a work to fulfill before Jesus would come. He knew his ministry was going to be short, and he didn't try to minister longer than God needed him to. When Jesus showed up, John said, "He must increase, but I must decrease" (John 3:30).

✗ It is so significant to understand that John the Baptist didn't fight to stay in charge of the hour. He allowed God's plan to unfold and Jesus to take over.

We need to follow John the Baptist's selfless example. It's important to know not only that times and seasons do change, but we must also recognize *when* they change and then accept with grace what our role is in the new season — even if it looks like we decrease as another takes center stage. We trust in God's faithfulness and in the wisdom of His plan.

GOD CHANGES THE TIMES AND SEASONS

And he changeth the times and the seasons: he removeth kings, and setteth up kings: he giveth wisdom unto the wise, and knowledge to them that know understanding.

Daniel 2:21

We must become sensitive and mature enough in the Spirit that when God changes the times and seasons to which we are accustomed, we do not get angry or upset. We must move with what God is doing, not against it. We cannot change times and seasons. We cannot even rearrange them. We cannot hold them still because God is the One who raises up and brings down.

When Daniel found himself in captivity in Babylon, he knew it was God's season for pruning rebellion and idolatry off His people through exile and life in a strange land. Yielding to the judgment as God told them to do would have allowed them to use the time of captivity for genuine repentance and changing of their ways. They could have been blessed in Babylon, and many were (*see* Jer. 29:4-14).

We must move with what God is doing, not against it. We cannot change times and seasons. We cannot even rearrange them.

He who keeps his command will experience nothing harmful; and a wise man's heart discerns both time and judgment.

Ecclesiastes 8:5 NKJV

A wise man knows both the timing of God and the judgment of God. A foolish person knows neither.

An immature Christian will cherish something beyond its time. A mature Christian will be joyful over change that is according to God's will.

A mature Christian knows God never brings His children down to a lower place — no matter how it looks on the outside. He always brings those who love and serve Him up to a better place. When it is *God's* change, it is always for the best.

SPIRITUAL HUNGER —
A DIVINE CATALYST

If you study the Scriptures and Church history, you'll find that one spiritual law remains consistent throughout: *Spiritual hunger is the catalyst that causes God to take us from one season to another.*

In Jesus' day, just as in our day, many were caught up in a past time. On the other hand, many others had a dissatisfaction ignited in their hearts. Those in the second category were sensitive to the things of God and sensed it was time for a change. There was no longer a peace found in relying on the letter of the Law that there had been. The desire for the Messiah to come had intensified in their hearts.

**Spiritual hunger is the catalyst
that causes God to take us
from one season to another.**

The Pharisees, on the other hand, fit in the first category — clinging to a past season of what God used to be doing. They also intensely wanted Messiah to come, but their desire came from their minds. Their "Messiah" had to fit their own concept and scenario — not God's. As a result, they missed Him when He came.

Today there is a hunger for truth — a hunger for the Word. Physical hunger is one of the most powerful drives on the earth because it directly relates to survival of the body. In the same way, spiritual hunger is one of the most powerful instincts in the Spirit realm because it supports the survival and growth of our spiritual walk.

When people are starving, they will do things that they otherwise would not do. They will eat things that in better times would not be acceptable at all.

The same is true in spiritual hunger. People are hungry for the written Word and for a direct, personal word from God. They are hungry for the fullness of the fivefold offices. They are so hungry to see God move that many times if they are not fed well spiritually, they try to fill their hunger through false prophecies and false prophets. Some try to take hold of the prophetic anointing themselves, separate from the call of God, and they end up making big mistakes.

I believe that a hunger for anything spiritual is a sign that God's time has changed. God's answer to the spiritual craving in the earth today is on its way. The truth is coming in stability and accuracy.

As we the Church continue to prepare our hearts, God will continue to mature His leaders who are called to proclaim what He desires to have said on the earth. By staying in the Word of God and prayer, we will all continue to sharpen our sensitivity and excel in maturity.

**A hunger for anything spiritual is a sign
that God's time has changed. God's answer
to the spiritual craving in the earth today is on its way.
The truth is coming in stability and accuracy.**

When you sense God changing the times and seasons of your life, don't resist Him. Change can be very exciting to those who are hungry for the Spirit of God. Don't get complacent in your time with God or too comfortable in your relationship with Him. Stay hungry for the things of God, and He will keep you in His perfect timing.

CHAPTER 3

A Time for Gifts, Revelations, and Offices

> ☆ A man has joy by the answer of his mouth, <u>and a word spoken in due season</u>, how good it is! ☆
>
> **Proverbs 15:23 NKJV**

In times of spiritual transition, the Church should always be seeking God to find His timing for what He has asked each one to do. Believers, and particularly those who are in ministry, should learn the times and the season they live in, for there are certain times for certain things to be spoken. A word spoken out of season brings more confusion than blessing, but a word spoken in season brings joy and clarity.

> The Lord God hath given me the tongue of the learned, that I should know how to speak a word in season to him that is weary....
>
> **Isaiah 50:4**

When we walk in the Spirit, we have the ability to speak the right words at the right time that will refresh, encourage, and rearrange the thinking of those who hear. That should always be our goal for the words we speak. God's words spoken in His timing will produce an atmosphere conducive to releasing more of the revelation that He has deposited within us and that He wants us to speak. But if we speak out in the wrong timing, our words can produce the opposite reaction in the hearts and minds of the listeners.

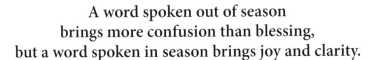

**A word spoken out of season
brings more confusion than blessing,
but a word spoken in season brings joy and clarity.**

When a believer speaks and delivers a revelation at the right time, it spreads like wildfire to fulfill God's purposes and further His plan. Many people speaking true words from God have gone through unnecessary persecution because the person delivering the message didn't understand to wait for His timing. Even a true word from God, given at the wrong time, can do much damage.

That's why it's so important that believers learn how to know when a word is "in season." So many just hear something and run with it, causing a negative reaction everywhere they go. Those people need an understanding of divine timing. Just because someone has a "word" doesn't mean it is to be delivered at that exact moment.

But the divine timing required to accomplish God's plan is only understood in the place of private communion with Him.

Many believers and ministries live in frustration because they try to analyze the timing of God through public opinion, intellect, or organization. As a result, they wear themselves out physically, emotionally, and spiritually. The ministry suddenly becomes a dreaded chore, followed by disillusionment and sin. Some have even left the ministry, feeling exhausted and seared.

The divine timing required to accomplish God's plan is only understood in the place of private communion with Him.

We need to know when to move and when to rest. Faith is now, but godly results are birthed from accurate timing.

The sign of a mature Christian is his ability to walk accurately in God's timing. A young Christian is characterized by his mistakes with timing. That does not mean he is always in deep trouble; it simply means he is in a time of spiritual training.

When I was learning this principle of spiritual timing, I would get a message in my heart and hold it. It was so much inside of me that I would stand in front of my mirror and speak it out to myself!

When you have a strong message from Heaven inside of you, it is alive — "kicking and moving," almost like an infant in the womb. You just want it to come forth and be born. You begin to ask the Lord, "When is it going to be time?" And if you're not careful, the message can become an irritation to you instead of a blessing.

But when a message from God burning on the inside of me comes out in His timing, it is always wonderful! The message goes out and lands in the hearts of people throughout the nations when I hit the right time of releasing that word.

 Everything the Holy Spirit gives belongs strategically in the sequential operations of divine timing. That's why revelation must be held for the accuracy of the Spirit's unction to release.

UNCTION OR EMOTION?

I've had prophecies for individuals that I wanted to give right at the moment I received the word. My soul said they needed to hear it, but in my spirit I had no release to give it. So I had to wait.

We must learn the difference between emotion and unction. We must speak out of the unction of the Spirit, not the pull of emotion.

An attempt to move in the Spirit by emotion will pull us out of the correct timing of God every time. Learning and operating with the unction in our spirit will keep us in step with His timing.

We must learn the difference between emotion and unction. We must speak out of the unction of the Spirit, not the pull of emotion.

The Greek word "charisma" means *an unguent or a smearing with oil or a salve.* It is usually translated as some form of the word "anoint."

The scholars who translated the *King James Version* of the Bible used "unction" as an English translation of *charisma* only one time in the entire Bible. "Unction" simply means *anointing*.

But ye have an unction from the Holy One, and ye know all things.

1 John 2:20

Do not give a prophecy to anyone unless you have the unction of the Holy Spirit to do so. There must be a divine stirring inside of you — it is *not* based on an emotion. It is not just a "good idea" to make the person feel better. That unction from God literally draws it out of you, for it is the unction, or anointing, that brings forth the prophecy in power.

Sometimes I have a prophecy in my spirit, and I walk into a meeting where the people seem to be really rejoicing and praising God, ready to receive — but there is no unction on me to bring forth the word. Then I go into another meeting where it doesn't look as if anything is happening, and *boom!* — here comes the unction to release the prophetic word.

I used to wonder why God would give a word at times to a less vocal group of people and not the group that was more demonstrative. Then I began to see that only God knows the hearts and the level of maturity of the people in a corporate setting. His prophecies are meant to begin a work immediately when they are received.

One of the fivefold offices is that of a prophet. Prophets must be very sensitive to the timing of the Holy Spirit. If they are not aware of the timing of God, they can become the trigger for self-induced persecution, simply because they released utterance without the unction of the Spirit or before the proper time.

Prophets are very aware of what God is doing today and in the future. But just because a prophet has the ability to "see" what God will do doesn't mean it is time for him to announce it — and it's *never* time for him to try to cause that word to happen. It is of utmost importance that prophets remain sensitive to the timing of God.

Some time ago, I became so tired of hearing "dead" prophecies that I thought if I heard one more, I would scream. Dead prophecies are exhortations out of someone's soul. They may be heartfelt, but they are not words from God and should not be given forth as such. No matter how good they sound or how scriptural they are, there is no anointing on those words when they are spoken in the form of prophecy.

If people are learning how to operate in the gifts or in the prophetic office, that is one thing. But some people have given out dead prophecies for years.

The unction from the Holy Spirit gives us power to speak the word of God with a high-ranking force that carries weight, rearranges people's thoughts, and shifts the direction they walk. Our emotions say that an exhortational prophecy means *"pat me."* But true biblical exhortation means *to urge, to admonish to push on*, and *to warn*.

The apostle Peter wrote that in former times, men of God spoke by the Holy Spirit, not by the will of men (*see* 2 Peter 1:21). New Testament times, including our present-day times, are no different. When a word is spoken in the correct timing with unction, it will come with weight, power, and force. The Holy Spirit knows the perfect time.

The unction from the Holy Spirit gives us power to speak the word of God with a high-ranking force that carries weight, rearranges people's thoughts, and shifts the direction they walk.

We must learn not to give forth a word just because an auditorium is full or the conditions seem right. It would be easy to release a word from the Lord when excitement runs high, but we must train ourselves to let the Holy Spirit lead us, not the excitement level in the room. The unction within will direct us to the appointed time.

TIME FOR THE PROPHETIC ANOINTING

I believe the heart and thrust of evangelism is a prophetic anointing. The greatest evangelists I have ever seen are those with the prophetic anointing. They are sensitive to the timing of God. They understand the seasons of God and the workings of the prophetic office. In fact, it is like two streams that converge together from different directions to form a mighty river. When the prophetic and the evangelistic streams meet head on by God's orchestration, they merge and produce divine power; they do not conflict.

Years ago, the Spirit of God began to bring out of me in prayer a call for the prophetic evangelist to come into the earth and to go through the nations reaping a harvest by saying and doing what God directs. I began to see the prophetic anointing come on some evangelists, but some tended to draw back because they were placed in arenas they were not accustomed to.

The natural side of people always wants to understand what is happening before stepping out. However, a believer learns some things simply by moving out in faith.

I saw one particular evangelist step out with the prophetic anointing, and the manifestation of God was very strong because he was sensitive to the shiftings and timings of the Holy Spirit. As he began to preach on the glory of God, that glory began to manifest in the room.

The natural side of people always wants to understand what is happening before stepping out. However, a believer learns some things simply by moving out in faith.

That is characteristic of someone functioning in the Holy Spirit's accurate timing with a prophetic anointing. What is preached or taught will be in demonstration as the minister steps out in faith.

As this evangelist preached, I could sense the glory of God come in the room. The stronger he preached, the stronger the glory became. His preaching was more like prophesying without saying, "Thus saith the Lord," in the middle of his sermon. He began this way: "The word of the Lord is..." Then the rest of the sermon was the word of the Lord.

Soon people all over the room began to weep. They began to come down the aisles without an altar call. Some of them ran to the altar. The glory of God and the conviction of the Holy Spirit were so strong that even those already saved wanted to be saved again! It was one of the most anointed meetings I had ever been in.

I believe all the fivefold offices are experiencing a new day with a prophetic anointing resting to a certain degree on many who stand in those offices. We are seeing prophetic pastors, prophetic teachers, and prophetic evangelists operating differently than we have been accustomed to in the past.

There have been prophetic evangelists in times past, because God's "new thing" is usually a restoration of something that has been lost or forgotten by the Church. John the Baptist was one who preached under a prophetic anointing, telling of things to come and warning of judgment at the same time he called people to repentance.

The anointing that John the Baptist operated under was what brought conviction. Otherwise, he would have been no different than other "wild men" of his day who spent solitary time in the desert and came out preaching. John's sensitivity to God's perfect timing, to the presence of the Holy Spirit, and to the prophetic anointing is what made him different.

TIMING WITH PRAISE AND WORSHIP

Over the past few decades, we have seen a prophetic anointing begin to influence praise and worship. Tradition is very strong in that arena of worship. Many churches have been delivered from the hymnbook but are now stuck on transparencies.

Some are still at the mercy of the machine that throws lyrics onto the wall or adheres to a systematic, preplanned song order.

The old songs were not the problem. "Religion" had crept in through a pattern of routinely singing the same old way in the flesh.

The newness of the songs fooled us. Because they were fresh, we could really get involved singing them. But new songs are not a substitute for the Holy Spirit's anointing, nor are they a sure sign of His anointing. New songs or old songs, it is the Holy Spirit's anointing upon the songs and the spirit in which we sing them that counts.

Some churches have set back their entire congregation because of the songs they sing before the message. The ministers leave frustrated, not understanding why the people couldn't grasp what they delivered to them. But too often the issue is the song service. It left the people stagnant and crusty, making it difficult for them to receive the full impact of the message.

We need to quit holding on to "the way we've always done it" in our church services just because that's our comfort zone. It's time to begin to move out into uncharted territory in God as we flow with the timing of the Spirit.

**We need to quit holding on
to "the way we've always done it" in our church services
just because that's our comfort zone. It's time to begin
to move out into uncharted territory in God
as we flow with the timing of the Spirit.**

LET THE HOLY SPIRIT LEAD THE SERVICE

Sometimes simple obedience will change the flow.

Years ago I was scheduled to speak at a certain church on Mother's Day. I usually have a word or a stirring in my spirit before I go to minister somewhere, but for this particular service, I wasn't picking up anything from the Lord. Before I left for the church, I looked up scriptures about mothers, and none of them were anointed to me. I walked into the pastor's office and said, "Pastor, I don't have anything for mothers today."

He said, "That's good, because I preached about mothers last week."

I thought, *Hallelujah! I don't have to worry about that.* But then the real problem came — I still didn't know what to preach. So I said, "I'll just go by faith."

The service began; the music started; and they were singing the usual Charismatic/Word of Faith songs. I was being nice and preferring my brethren, being very sweet and respectful — but then the Lord said to me, *"I want you to dance."* So I began doing a nice little Charismatic "wiggle," but the Holy Spirit spoke to my heart and said, *"No, no, no!"*

"Well, what do You want then?" I asked.

He said, *"I want the old combined with the new."*

I said, "Oh. You mean, don't 'wiggle' but *dance*."

The Spirit of God answered, *"Yes."*

Now, at that time I was still coming out of tradition as fast as I could, but I have to admit that there was a little bit left. I was further than some people, but there were still some things I was dealing with.

I said, "But Lord, it's Mother's Day! Everyone is wearing flowers." I knew God was going to do a work in that place, but I also knew that everyone was dressed up with flowers pinned to their dresses. And with visitors there, no one wanted to sweat — after all, it was Mother's Day!

But when the Lord says *"dance"* to me, I know that doesn't mean the normal Charismatic two-step. That means *dance*. When I dance, I get into it all over. I am everywhere.

Well, I started to dance.

Here's another thing you have to understand when you're learning to obey the promptings and timings of the Spirit of God. On the way up into the Spirit realm, you have to fight demons, whether you're obeying Him in prayer or praise and worship.

In this case, half of the front row, including a member of my staff, went with me. As soon as I began to really dance, I was in a fight. This was not one of those "bringing-down-the-glory" dances; it was a *"we-are-going-to-win"* dance. There was a controlling spirit dominating that church, and God wanted them set free.

Sometimes we get into places that we know very little about. We must know the accurate timings of God in order to move correctly with what His Spirit intends to do.

We were singing a praise song full of zeal, and the atmosphere was being flooded with the praises of the people. Suddenly the musicians started to change over to a worship song — but it wasn't the time to move from a praise song into a quiet worship song.

The unction was strong in me, and I said, "*Don't do it!* Go back to that other song, and let's sing it some more."

**Sometimes we get into places
that we know very little about.
We must know the accurate timings of God
in order to move correctly with what
His Spirit intends to do.**

We went back to the first song, and people all over the building began to enter in with us — all except the musicians. Because they hadn't been sensitive to the timing of God, they remained startled that their systematic order had been changed. They were trying to be nice and sweet, but the Holy Spirit wanted to move among the people and the musicians weren't cooperating.

I finally moved over and stood right in the middle of the instrumentalists. They looked petrified, but I kept telling them, "*Play with force! Play with force!*" Finally, they hit it with force. For two and a half hours, we sang, danced, and sweated, and that controlling spirit came down that day. That church was set free.

The service was noisy, yet decent and in order. What most people call "decently and in order" means organizing the Holy Spirit right out of the service. But that's not it at all.

Freedom for that church didn't come by preaching or prophesying. *Freedom came by being sensitive to God's chosen way for the hour.* It came to that congregation by allowing the

Holy Spirit to do His work, and it came by the minstrel and the dance.

We must be careful not to learn from a "system." We must continually fine-tune our ability to learn from the unction of the Holy Spirit, or we will become religious. God wants us to move under His unction, not by performance or by "working things up" through emotion and the flesh.

Some musicians and song leaders sing and play only out of their heads; they're not sensitive to the leading of the Holy Spirit. Many of their gifts are being aborted, because they choose to operate completely in the flesh through intellect and organization. It is so sad to see a worship leader in bondage to a system.

**We must be careful not to learn from a "system."
We must continually fine-tune our ability to learn
from the unction of the Holy Spirit,
or we will become religious.**

I don't know music, but I do know how to lead praise and worship in the Spirit. At times an anointing, an unction, comes on me to be able to do this. I must hear the timing of God in each service that I minister in.

We must learn to operate from the unction and the timing of God, for it will lead to godly results every time.

CHAPTER 4

Pitfalls of Wrong Timing

K ing David was a man after God's own heart (*see* 1 Sam. 13:14). Yet he is a classic example of a leader of God's people who missed the spiritual timing of the hour.

Second Samuel 11 records a tragic incident in David's life. In past years when I preached on that chapter, I used it as a text for a message on sexual misconduct. However, later on an airplane flying home from Europe, the Lord prompted me to reread the account. Then He asked me a question: *"Why did David commit these sins at this particular time?"*

I answered the Lord with my usual thoughts on David's misconduct with Bathsheba. He answered me, *"Read it again."*

And it came to pass, after the year was expired, at the time when kings go forth to battle, that David sent Joab, and

his servants with him, and all Israel; and they destroyed the children of Ammon, and besieged Rabbah. But David tarried still at Jerusalem.

2 Samuel 11:1

The Lord asked me, "What time was it?"

I replied, "It was the end of the year."

The Lord said, *"That is not the time I am talking about. That is natural time. What time was it otherwise?"*

I answered, "Well, that verse says it was the time when kings go forth to battle."

That was it! The sins for which David is so remembered are only the surface of the core issue — *he missed the timing that God ordained for him to follow.*

Where was David at a time when the kings went forth into battle? Where was the king when his men were out fighting for their nation and taking territory that the Lord had promised? God gave land to them, but they had to occupy it. But instead of leading the fight for the Lord, David sent his men to fight while he stayed home. This was very unusual behavior for a king.

**The sins for which David is so remembered
are only the surface of the core issue —
*he missed the timing that
God ordained for him to follow.***

When people don't operate in God's timing for them, they are vulnerable to the traps and temptations of the enemy. David ultimately committed adultery and murder because he didn't go with his men into battle, thus missing the timing of God.

Missing God's timing is as dangerous as being deliberately disobedient. David had removed himself from underneath the shelter of His wings.

The same thing can happen to us to one degree or another. I believe the degree is linked to how much we are aware of God's timing. He will never leave us, but we quite often walk away from Him. He is still our Father, yet we're not in the close fellowship that is necessary to be in tune with Him. And when we are out of tune with the Spirit of God, we aren't as sensitive to His voice. We don't hear Him as clearly when He warns us of things to come.

Hosea 4:6 speaks of God's people being destroyed through lack of knowledge. David's lack of insight, which caused him not to realize that missing God's timing might destroy him, almost did exactly that.

When we are out of tune with the Holy Spirit, we aren't as sensitive to His voice. We don't hear Him as clearly when He warns us of things to come.

Some may say, "But David's main problem was not spending enough time in prayer or communion with God."

Yet even prayer and studying the Word cannot substitute adequately for your obedience according to God's direction and His time. What prayer and reading the Word *will* do, however, is make it more likely that you will hear the Holy Spirit if you are not in the right place or if you're not in step with His timing. And once you discern the Spirit's correction, you'll be more likely to allow Him to realign you with His will for you.

THE PITFALL OF PRIDE

David was a strong leader, anointed and chosen by God — so how did he miss the timing of God? As I went on to study 2 Samuel, I saw some major character flaws in David at this particular point in his life.

The main root of David's problem at this time was pride. Any leader who is in true, humble authority will be with his people and not on a manmade pedestal. David placed himself on a pedestal by refusing to be in the battle with his people. After all, he was the king and he could do whatever he wanted, with whom he wanted, whenever he wanted. He could invent his own rules and regulations if he so desired.

David had the position, the money, the power, the comfort, the reputation, and the respect. The people already knew he was a great warrior. He no longer felt he had to maintain that reputation because it was firmly established.

Although God gave David these blessings, David chose at this particular time to set himself up as his own law. He chose to remain in the king's palace, comfortable and safe, rather than be with his men in battle. David didn't realize that setting himself outside the spiritual timing of God was deadlier than any natural weapon on the battleground.

The main reason we might knowingly walk out from the correct timing of God is to get our own way. When we don't walk in the Spirit and our hearts are not submitted to the will of God, the only thing left to lead us is our carnal desires.

David didn't realize that setting himself outside the spiritual timing of God was deadlier than any natural weapon on the battleground.

And it came to pass in an evening tide, that David arose from off his bed, and walked upon the roof of the kings house: and from the roof he saw a woman washing herself; and the woman was very beautiful to look upon.

2 Samuel 11:2

When we are not submitted to the timing of God, peace leaves and restlessness comes.

David's mind was obviously racing with thoughts. Driven from sleep by his active mind, he got up, walked out on the roof one night, and caught a glimpse of a beautiful woman bathing. All of the men in Israel should have been out in battle. The woman was within her rights to bathe, believing that no man was left in the city.

When a person is out of the will and the timing of God, his mind isn't set on the things of Heaven. In that moment of seeing Bathsheba, David's own desire consumed him, and he became obsessed with the thought of conquering her.

Because of David's intense pride at that time and his lust of the moment, it no longer mattered to him what was right or wrong. It no longer mattered that Bathsheba was another man's wife. It didn't even matter to David that her husband was Uriah

51

the Hittite, <u>one of his most faithful servants</u> (*see* 2 Sam. 11:8-13). All that mattered to David was that his desire be fulfilled, no matter the cost.

When a person is out of the will and the timing of God, his mind isn't set on the things of Heaven.

It is sad to say, but when people reach this point, they are usually capable of any and all sin, because their conscience has been seared. I have seen friends and ministers in this condition who fell because of their uncontrolled desire, with some losing all that they had previously given their entire lives for.

So there David was — in the wrong place at the wrong time — and as a result, he yielded to his own fleshly desire.

And David sent messengers, and took her; and she came in unto him, and he lay with her; for she was purified from her uncleanness: and she returned unto her house. And the woman conceived, and sent and told David, and said, I am with child.

2 Samuel 11:4-5

Instead of repenting for what he had done, David fell deeper into sin to cover his selfish actions. He turned into another man, one totally opposite of the character that God had exalted in him. David began to plot, scheme, and lie to cover his error. He began to betray his people and his household by pretending to be something he wasn't.

When uncontrolled desire consumes a person, normalcy leaves. It almost seems as if common sense is nowhere to be found. Extreme behavior patterns surface because the desire has become so great that the sense of right and wrong has been numbed and suppressed.

Those who have reached this stage of desire will cut off association with all those around them who have a different standard and will gather others to themselves who support their ways. Some even twist Scripture and its principles to justify their actions. Uncontrolled desire has blinded them from the need to pursue the timing of God and a close relationship with Him.

Missing God's timing as a result of selfish desire causes people to devour anything that stands in their way. When they step out of His proper timing, it means they step into every vice that can accompany the wrong. When uncontrolled desire leads a life without repentance, acts of betrayal, lying, stealing, cheating, lust, and eventually physical death can follow.

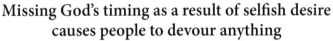

**Missing God's timing as a result of selfish desire
causes people to devour anything
that stands in their way.**

David followed this dangerous pattern. He attempted to deceive and flatter Uriah, the woman's husband, in order to convince him to go home and sleep with his wife so it would appear that the baby was his. But Uriah was so faithful and trusting of David's kindness that he vowed even deeper loyalty to his country. He refused to lie with his wife when the rest of his comrades were still fighting on the battlefield.

Out of desperation and with a total disregard of right or wrong, David ordered Uriah to be sent to the front lines of the battle. David knew that with this order, he was sending Uriah to his death (*see* 2 Sam. 11:6-24).

LOVING COMFORT MORE THAN OBEDIENCE

David had to face another area of pride in his heart that caused him to miss the timing of God — he had become *too comfortable.*

David was surrounded by people who said *yes* to whatever he dictated. Because his heart had become turned by comfort, he used those whom God had sent to him for his own gain and protection.

If you don't surround yourself with those who can sharpen you like iron, you are setting yourself up for a great fall.

I have seen many friends and ministers pad themselves inside a group of "yes men" because it comforts them. But here is the problem: Should one of these ministers fall into sin, seasoned leaders in the Body can't hear their cry for help because the "padding" around them — made up of those who unquestioningly reinforce their own faulty conclusions — is so thick.

**If you don't surround yourself with those
who can sharpen you like iron,
you are setting yourself up for a great fall.**

We cannot stay accurate if we surround ourselves with unreality. When we allow ourselves to stay cushioned and comfortable, we lose our cutting edge. Loving comfort above all else will rob us of hitting the timing of God. If we run from confrontation because we fear it might shake our comfort zone, we are heading straight into defeat.

That doesn't mean to say that clinging to one's comfort zone necessarily throws that person into sexual sin. For instance, some people fall prey to religious spirits. They are often the ones who get easily offended.

Sin comes in many forms. Everybody has areas of greater temptation. But a person who loves his comfort over his own character development makes himself more vulnerable to yield to temptation in those areas.

If we run from confrontation because we fear it might shake our comfort zone, we are heading straight into defeat.

A minister once said to me, "Well, Roberts, I believe that all we need to do is just preach the Gospel." Well, I believe that too. But there is more to the Gospel than just giving it out whatever way we want to. There is an accuracy in timing and delivery that we must learn to hit every time, and godly character is one of the items on our checklist that teaches us that accuracy.

Many who like comfort zones will not like this book. Learning to deepen one's spiritual hunger while walking in God's timing requires a willingness to accept responsibility and a certain level of pressure that comes with pursuing His will. Comfort-loving people want to set both of these requirements aside.

How does a person come to a place in life where he or she loves comfort more than God? There are several causes. One is sin in the heart:

> **For all that is in the world — the lust of the flesh [craving for sensual gratification] and the lust of the eyes [greedy longings of the mind] and the pride of life [assurance in one's own resources or in the stability of earthly things] — these do not come from the Father but are from the world [itself].**
>
> **1 John 2:16 AMPC**

The way this verse describes the pride of life sounds a clear warning to all: Man is not to rely on the "assurance in one's own resources or in the stability of earthly things." These are not of God, but of the world, and they will cause a person to love comfort more than the Father.

Many lose their focus when they become more comfortable with a maintenance ministry than moving forward in alignment with what God is doing today. But times and seasons all come to an end, and new ones always begin. If a person gets caught in the wrong place at the wrong time because it's "comfortable," a tendency to yield to sin can begin to settle in, which can lead to a state of captivity.

TRUTH IS OFTEN UNCOMFORTABLE

Sometimes breaking new ground — going where people have not gone in ways that seem untraditional — can get a person into trouble with his peers. When it comes to ministry, some fear that being different than other churches will hurt their church growth.

Many pastors today are very selective about the subjects they will preach about. They don't want to preach anything that might be the least bit offensive to their congregations. But like it or not, the truth is often offensive and uncomfortable. MESSY

When we read the stories of the men and women who did great exploits in the Bible, we can see by their lives that they certainly didn't seek comfort or security above the will of God. Neither did these men and women live in comfortable, stable, and secure times.

So if you begin to sense God moving in a different way than you have been used to seeing, accept it. Don't reject His leading or hold it at arm's length away from you. On the other hand, test every spirit by the Word of God. It isn't wise to go to the other extreme and think, *Well, this is a different direction, so it must be from God!*

You may be trying to make your life fit into the way you have it planned. But to move accurately in the timings of God, you have to be willing to see your plans turned upside down from the way you originally thought.

Years ago, the Lord taught me something very important that has kept me out of the comfort zone. He said, *"Don't try to live your life according to what other people do."* I have learned to live my life two ways: according to the timing of God and according to the calling upon my life.

On the other hand, allowing people to think you are special because of doing things God's way is also a trap of the devil to hinder you.

Because I endeavored to follow God's timing and live my life differently than many others my age, people called me *unique.* I didn't know how to respond to that, so I would agree that I was different.

Then the Lord said to me, *"Quit agreeing with a lie! You're not a unique case. That will open a door of pride if you keep saying that. Because you are walking in My time, what is happening in your life is normal. It is not unique, peculiar, nor an oddity. Your life is normal."*

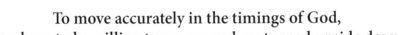

**To move accurately in the timings of God,
you have to be willing to see your plans turned upside down
from the way you originally thought.**

From Heaven's perspective, people who obey God are normal. People who walk in His timing are normal. Those who don't know spiritual time and walk in the timings of the world are the ones who are different and out of step with God's ways.

Other people used to tell me I was strange, and I would say, "Yes, I know, but I'm changing." After the Lord began to talk to me about that as well, I had to stop agreeing. I began to say, "No, I'm not weird or strange; I'm actually normal. I just know how to walk in God's timing for my life."

Christians who are single particularly need to look for God's timing in connection with marriage. Loneliness and insecurity can be great pitfalls and have caused too many to miss the timing of God.

Even if you know the one you are to marry, there is a correct timing. The Holy Spirit told me, *"There are going to be many people in this day who will come close to aborting their callings because of trying on their own to make things happen in the area of marriage."*

Choosing comfort over God's will and His ways puts people in danger of being taken captive in their own world. This is true whether it means coming against a move of God, coming against the word of the Lord, or coming against the brethren that might not believe exactly like they do.

So don't allow people or circumstances to put you in a box or place you in a certain slot and keep you there. Have faith that God knows what He is doing, and keep your mind under control. Don't allow your mind to move you from the timing of God and the place where He has positioned you.

**Don't allow your mind to move you
from the timing of God and the place
where He has positioned you.**

Lacking a Heart for People

David's actions in 2 Samuel 11 reveal a third character flaw: a lack of heart for his people.

Then David said unto the messenger, Thus shalt thou say unto Joab [concerning the planned death of Uriah]**, Let not this thing displease thee, for the sword devoureth one as well as another: make thy battle more strong against the city, and overthrow it: and encourage thou him.**

2 Samuel 11:25

Whether or not we hold a position of leadership, when we have a heart for people, we will listen to Heaven and be by their side through good times and bad.

David sent the people out to face difficult times alone because he felt superior to them at that time. But as he stayed behind, he fell into sin.

One of the saddest sights in the world is a minister who has lost his or her heart for people. When people lose their heart for the human race and turn that desire toward themselves, sin will eventually devastate them. They will become absorbed in their own selfish pursuits, unable to minister to others.

Throughout the Old Testament, God showed Himself strong on behalf of the people. Although the prophets were appalled by the sin of the people, they didn't turn away from them in their hearts. Instead, the prophets would rend their own garments and cry out in repentance on behalf of the people as if they had sinned themselves.

When people lose their heart for the human race and turn that desire toward themselves, sin will eventually devastate them.

The prophet Jonah had a difficult time learning that kind of compassion for people. He thought the people of Nineveh should reap the punishment they deserved. But God taught this prophet a hard lesson, and in the end, Jonah obeyed God and warned the people to repent (*see* Jonah chapters 1-4).

Moses constantly considered the people over himself. Even with the great tasks he had to face, only once did he turn his heart against the people, reacting in anger and accusation. He disobeyed God, called the people a very accurate name, and then struck the rock twice instead of just speaking to it as God had commanded. And as a result of this one serious mistake of Moses, God didn't allow him to enter the Promised Land (*see* Num. 20:1-13). God takes the representation of His heart toward people very seriously.

Gideon was one who had a heart for the people.

> **And the angel of the Lord appeared unto him, and said unto him, The Lord is with thee, thou mighty man of valour.**
>
> **Judges 6:12**

Where would your heart be if the angel of the Lord appeared to you and told you the Lord was with you? Look at Gideon's heart:

> **And Gideon said unto him, Oh my Lord, if the Lord be with us, why then is all this befallen us? and where be all his miracles which our fathers told us of saying, Did not the Lord bring us up from Egypt? but now the Lord bath forsaken us, and delivered us into the hands of the Midianites.**
>
> **Judges 6:13**

Gideon didn't single himself out from the people. He didn't stick out his chest, puff himself up, and say, "I've got it. I have arrived. Yes, I am chosen; God is with me. Stick with me, and you will make it," No, he answered with his heart — his heart for the people.

> **And the Lord looked upon him, and said, Go in this thy might, and thou shalt save Israel from the hand of the Midianites: have not I sent thee?**
>
> **Judges 6:14**

These words from the Lord were very significant. The might of Gideon to which the Lord referred was his *heart* for *the people* and *his heart for miracles.* These two ingredients added together produce a sensitivity to the correct timings of God.

**God takes the representation
of His heart toward people very seriously.**

The Lord went on to tell Gideon in verse 16 that Gideon and the people would smite the enemy as *one man.* When leadership and believers have a heart for one another, a unity is forged that the work of darkness cannot penetrate. The Body of Christ is invincible when unified in heart.

Many verses show the heart of Jesus while He walked on the earth, but one in particular expresses how timing and a heart for the people walk hand in hand.

> **Now before the feast of the passover, when Jesus knew that his hour was come that he should depart out of this**

world unto the Father, having loved his own which were in the world, he loved them unto the end.

John 13:1

Jesus knew His time to leave this world had come. But notice the last part of that verse: "…Having loved his own which were in the world, he loved them unto the end."

The very people Jesus had come to redeem persecuted, beat, and rejected Him. Even His own disciples betrayed, deserted, and lied about Him! Yet Jesus' heart remained fixed on the benefit of all mankind, even to His death. Like Abraham, Jesus remained "…fully assured that what God had promised, He was able also to perform" (Rom. 4:21 NASB). As a result, at the appointed time, Jesus triumphantly fulfilled the plan of the Father for all eternity.

So whatever God has called you to do, whether it is to lead or to follow, do it with a heart for people. Don't let pride or comfort prevent you from fulfilling the perfect plan of God at the perfect time. When God says, "Go" — go! When God says, "Wait," wait. Don't become impatient; just keep trusting in the Lord and in His ways.

Don't let pride or comfort prevent you from fulfilling the perfect plan of God at the perfect time.

CHAPTER 5

Blessings of
Right Timing

Learning to obey the Holy Spirit's leading and flow in His timings is an absolutely essential part of finding and fulfilling God's plan for your life.

Just as we have discussed character flaws that can cause us to miss God's timing, we need to take a look at some attributes that cause us to *align* with His timing.

**Learning to obey the Holy Spirit's leading
and flow in His timings is an absolutely essential part
of finding and fulfilling God's plan for your life.**

One of the most successful stories in the Bible concerning two people who operated in the correct timing of God was Esther and Mordecai. Esther's name means "star," and as far as I am concerned, she gets one in my book.

SUBMITTING TO GODLY AUTHORITY

In the Old Testament book of Esther, an interesting story unfolds. King Ahasuerus had just relieved Queen Vashti of her royal duties and proclaimed the call for a new queen throughout the region (*see* Esther 2:1-4).

Mordecai's uncle had died and left a daughter, Esther, whom Mordecai had taken in and raised as his own. Esther became one of the many women brought into the palace to stand before the king (*see* Esther 2:7-8).

Although Esther was on her own in the palace, Mordecai asked her to not reveal that she was a Jew. Keeping this secret wasn't deceptive; Mordecai simply sensed that it wasn't yet the time to reveal it. He was a man of wisdom — a quality that caused him to be exalted later on. Esther's submission to Mordecai's authority and godly advice enabled her to enter into God's correct timing and fulfill her appointed role to save the entire Jewish nation from destruction (*see* Esther 2:10-23).

Godly authority is designed to be our protection and covering. Submitting to the godly authority God places over us creates a strength inside of us and gives us the added courage to walk in obedience. What we do then is ordained by God and not appointed by a friend or an idea.

In Numbers 16, Korah and those most popular in the camp made the fatal assumption that they had a right to exert as much authority over the people as Moses and Aaron did. They murmured the same complaint we hear today from those who should know better: "We are just as holy as you, and we can hear God for ourselves. Who do you think you are, trying to be the leader?" (*see* Num. 16:2-3).

Submitting to the godly authority God places over us creates a strength inside of us and gives us the added courage to walk in obedience.

Every New Testament believer has the ability and the unction within to hear from God for themselves concerning themselves. But God has ordained some to be set in the fivefold ministry to fulfill specific ministry roles in leading, equipping, and training the Body of Christ (*see* Eph. 4:11-16). Jesus is the One who gave these gifts to the Body. He gave them titles — apostle, prophet, evangelist, pastor, and teacher — and equipped each to fulfill specific functions. However, all have a common function: to mature the saints and teach them how to hear God for themselves so they will not be deceived (*see* Eph. 4:12-15).

The responsibility and pressure that accompany a call to one of these ministry gifts can be staggering at times. Many of those called into the fivefold ministry never sought or desired the position.

The apostle Paul went on to explain what we do once we understand the function of the fivefold ministry gifts:

This I say therefore, and testify in the Lord, that ye henceforth walk not as other Gentiles [or carnal ones] **walk, in the vanity** [emptiness] **of their mind, having the understanding darkened, being alienated from the life of God through the ignorance that is in them, because of the blindness of their heart.**

Ephesians 4:17-18

Do you see what Paul was saying? If we walk in our own ways, not submitted to authority, we won't know the timing of God for our lives because our disobedience opens the door to the spiritual darkness and blindness that surrounds us in the world. For us as believers, being alienated from the life of God means not walking according to His time and season. Abundant life is made available to us as we walk closely with God, but we cannot walk in that abundant life while we're out of His timing.

We are not to put those in leadership on a pedestal, but we are to respect and honor them for teaching and equipping us to fulfill God's plan for our lives. By honoring our leaders and learning from their lives and ministries, our hearts become more sensitive to the correct seasons of God. As a result, maturity and blessings follow us.

**Abundant life is made available to us
as we walk closely with God,
but we cannot walk in that abundant life
while we're out of His timing.**

It is imperative that we as Christians — and that includes Christian leaders — submit ourselves to godly authority in this hour so that the Holy Spirit can accomplish His plan through us.

MOTIVES MUST BE RIGHT

After Esther was chosen to be a maiden in the palace, it was time for her to be brought before the king. The palace had a set regulation that whatever the maiden asked for or desired was to be given to her (*see* Esther 2:13). Such a broad ruling would certainly expose the greed or lack of it in a person's heart! The remaining maidens must have asked for much, for in verse 15, we hear how Esther stood out as different when her appointed time came to be presented to the king.

> **Now when the turn of Esther, the daughter of Abihail the uncle of Mordecai, who had taken her for his daughter, was come to go in unto the king, she required nothing but what Hegai the king's chamberlain, the keeper of the women, appointed....**
>
> **Esther 2:15**

Verse 15 goes on to describe the result of a right motive:

> **...And Esther obtained favour in the sight of all them that looked upon her.**

To obtain the favor of God along the path of divine purpose, believers must have correct heart motives. Many people have attempted to cover their motives through flattery or deception, but the truth always comes to light.

In this hour, time is speeding up because the end is drawing near. That means the works of men come to light in a quicker way — good and bad. The right motive, even when we make a mistake, will protect us and keep us sensitive to the heart of God. We need to continuously check our motives and stay tuned to the Holy Spirit.

Some time ago, I was in a meeting with pastors and teachers, and they were talking about how "everyone thinks they are prophets today." Finally, they asked me what I thought — so I decided to get bold.

The right motive, even when we make a mistake, will protect us and keep us sensitive to the heart of God.

I replied, "Your motives aren't right. The reason ministers often get so touchy about the subject of prophets is that they are nervous for their own ministries and pastorates.

"If you talk about something happening in the Church in the right spirit, there is no criticism. You can be cautious, but you will not be judgmental of some other person in the Body or come against something God is doing. That kind of discussion with the right motive is led by the Holy Spirit. It brings truth and an earnest seeking of God's help.

"Something is wrong with the way you're all talking about prophets and the restoration of that office," I told this group of ministers. "Remember the healing revival? Remember how many people misused the gifts? Remember the extremes that people went to — no doctors, no medicine, and so forth? Why didn't you throw out the foundational principle of healing when those errors and false manifestations began to occur?

"And what about the faith movement and all of those on the fringes who got into presumption? Why didn't you throw out the faith message?

"And then there's the message of prosperity," I continued. "What about all those who misunderstood that message and gave money from selfish motives, believing only for their new car or new house? Why didn't you throw out the prosperity message? You didn't because there was still truth in the middle of error. There was a pure revelation from God mixed in there somewhere.

"So right now, God is restoring deliverance, intercession, and the prophetic," I concluded. "Yes, some imbalance is going to surface, but are you going to throw out the purity of God's truth along with the flesh and the demonic influences that try to get involved? Are you going to throw out the baby with the bathwater?"

I pray the ministers received what the Holy Spirit was saying in that response. Otherwise, they were in danger of missing God's timing and season for the days ahead because they didn't respond when the Lord was dealing with wrong motives in their hearts.

"Are you going to throw out the purity of God's truth along with the flesh and the demonic influences that try to get involved? Are you going to throw out the baby with the bathwater?"

Your motives must not only be right in ministry, but also in studying and talking about the ministry entrusted to others. Pray for those in error, but don't gossip or talk negatively about them. They are God's servants to straighten out, not yours (*see* Rom. 14:4).

Esther's motive was not to take the riches and heap them upon herself. Her motive was to be obedient and to respect the king and his palace. As a result, the king favored her above all the women and placed the crown of a queen upon her head (*see* Esther 2:17).

Because Esther displayed a pure and humble motive, she received the king's favor that exalted her to a place of position and authority. Her strong character allowed God to strategically place her as His agent of deliverance when the enemy attempted to destroy the Jewish people. Esther did her part while she was in her place at the right time — and, as a result, the lives of her people were spared.

✶ PRAYER AND FASTING — ✶ THE PRICE AND THE POWER SOURCE ✶

Prayer is the price and the power source of a Spirit-filled life pursuing God's timing and strategies for fulfilling His purpose. I will not attempt to cover all the benefits of prayer in this book, but I do want to bring out how fasting and prayer prepared Esther to accomplish her task.

Prayer is the vehicle of travel in the Spirit. Its steering wheel is the Word of God, and its fuel is your persistence. There is no wall too thick for prayer to plow through. Prayer is absolutely vital to your spiritual strength.

We see in Esther chapters 3 and 4 that King Ahasuerus had promoted the wicked Haman over all the princes of the region. Haman had a pride problem, and he did not like the fact that Mordecai refused to bow down to him. Once Haman discovered that Mordecai was a Jew, he decided to destroy the entire

Jewish nation. The king unknowingly granted his consent, and the decree was published throughout the region (*see* Esther 3:5-15).

**Prayer is the vehicle of travel in the Spirit.
Its steering wheel is the Word of God,
and its fuel is your persistence.**

Mordecai sent word to Esther, telling her to reveal her Jewish nationality to the king. Esther replied that she had not been summoned by the king in 30 days, and anyone who entered the inner court of the palace would be put to death unless the king raised the golden scepter.

Mordecai responded:

> **"...If you remain completely silent at this time, relief and deliverance will arise for the Jews from another place, but you and your father's house will perish. Yet who knows whether you have come to the kingdom for such a time as this?"**

Esther 4:14 NKJV

There will always be certain people who will rise at a certain time, anointed to speak a particular message or do a certain work. Just as God appointed Esther to be a deliverer, so He will call upon many in this hour to rise up and become deliverers in the power of His Spirit for *this* generation.

How do you make sure you are positioned correctly to do your part accurately in the timing of the Lord? Develop godly character, cultivate a strong spirit through the Word and through prayer and fasting, and maintain intimate fellowship with the Father. These are the essentials in your walk with Him that will empower you and position you to know exactly what you are to do and when and where you are to do it — nothing less.

**There will always be certain people
who will rise at a certain time,
anointed to speak a particular message
or do a certain work.**

Gideon was an example of someone who understood that he had just one job. In Judges 8:23 (NKJV), the people pleaded with him to rule over them and be their king because of his success in overcoming their enemies. But Gideon knew his place, his position, and the season of God. He answered, "...I will not rule over you, nor shall my son rule over you; the Lord shall rule over you." Gideon's job was to bring deliverance and help to the nation. And once he had fulfilled his assignment, Gideon didn't try to be more than what God had called him to be.

Ecclesiastes 3:1 says, "To every thing there is a season, and a time to every purpose under the heaven."

In response to Mordecai's exhortation, Esther rose up in her spirit and accepted her position for the hour. She instructed Mordecai and all of the Jews with him to fast and pray for three days — no food or water. She and her maidens vowed to do the same (*see* Esther 4:16).

There is a correct season and an appointed time to come forth and do the job you are being positioned to do. Prayer and fasting will keep you alert to God's plan.

To experience the supernatural realm of God, we must be adventurous in prayer. I am sure that Esther and the Jewish nation ventured out to a high level of prayer, because great understanding came for the path to victory.

**There is a correct season and an appointed time
to come forth and do the job you are being positioned to do.
Prayer and fasting will keep you alert to God's plan.**

Esther received detailed instructions on how to win the favor of the king for the Jewish nation. After the three days of prayer and fasting, Esther invited the king and Haman to dinner. The king graciously accepted, as did Haman, thinking he was being favored. Once there, the king begged Esther to tell him what she desired of him.

Instead of Esther blurting out all she knew before it was the right time, she had built discipline through her godly character and her prayer and fasting. She told the king nothing; instead, she invited the king and Haman back for a second banquet the following night.

When they returned the next night, the king's heart was ready to hear all that his queen would ask of him. Esther explained the dire situation to him, revealing that Haman had plotted the destruction of the Jews. Because of Esther's courage and strategic timing, not only were Haman and his sons hung on the gallows that Haman had prepared for Mordecai, but his enemy Mordecai was exalted and made second only to the king (*see* Esther 5:7-8:2).

Through Esther's strength in God and her wisdom in following His timing, she fully executed her part in His plan. She not only rid her people of the main enemy, the man named Haman, but his ten sons — the next generation raised to continue his evil agenda — were executed as well (*see* Esther 9:13).

That is the anointing and the spiritual power of those who walk in the timing of God. They will not stop at the first phase of victory; they pursue until the entire problem is conquered.

But the story doesn't end there. Being accurate in the timing of God produces a harvest of souls. After the victory was proclaimed throughout the region, conviction came to the people.

> **...And many of the people of the land became Jews; for the fear of the Jews fell upon them.**
>
> **Esther 8:17**

To this day, the Jewish people celebrate the victory God granted their nation through Esther and Mordecai.

**That is the anointing and the spiritual power
of those who walk in the timing of God.
They will not stop at the first phase of victory;
they pursue until the entire problem is conquered.**

First Chronicles 12:32 speaks "...of the children of Issachar, which were men that had understanding of the times, to know what Israel ought to do...." The word "understanding" in the Hebrew means to *perceive.*[1]

---

[1] James Strong, *Hebrew and Chaldee Dictionary*, 20, #995 and #998.

It is the will of God that you perceive in your spirit the spiritual time you are in and that you know the job you are to accomplish within that time. When you are submitted to the time and season God has for you — watch out! You are about to be enriched with abundant blessings from Heaven, overwhelmed with the favor of both God and man, and anointed to produce the results that God has assigned you to accomplish.

Walking in God's will according to His timing empowers us to produce total victory in every area — every time. The sick are healed; the oppressed go free; the lost are saved; the enemy is defeated; and the Kingdom progresses to the glory of God!

**Walking in the will of God
according to His timing
empowers us to produce total victory
in every area — every time.**

Part 2

THE QUEST
FOR SPIRITUAL
HUNGER

CHAPTER

Developing
a Spiritual Hunger

Blessed are those who hunger and thirst for righteousness, for they shall be filled.

Matthew 5:6 NKJV

How do we learn to flow in the timings and seasons of God? This verse in Matthew provides one of the keys: *to cultivate a deep hunger to know God and His ways.*

An incident that occurred in Jesus' life when He was a young boy provides us with a vivid example of what spiritual hunger looks like. In keeping with Jewish custom, Jesus' parents went to Jerusalem for the Feast of the Passover every year. When Jesus was 12 years old, His family made their annual trip to Jerusalem for the feast. When the feast was over, Jesus' parents started the return trip home, unaware that their Son wasn't with them.

Jesus had stayed behind in Jerusalem because of His great interest in the affairs of His Heavenly Father. Even at the tender age of 12, Jesus hungered for the things of the Spirit of God.

Thinking that Jesus was somewhere in their company, His parents traveled on for a day. Finally realizing that He wasn't with them, they began looking among their relatives and friends, and when they didn't find Jesus, they returned to Jerusalem.

ATTENDING TO THE FATHER'S BUSINESS

After three days, Mary and Joseph found their Son in the Temple courts, sitting among the teachers, listening to them and asking them questions. Everyone who heard Jesus was amazed at His understanding of the Scriptures.

> **When his parents saw him, they were astonished. His mother said to him, "Son, why have you treated us like this? Your father and I have been anxiously searching for you."**
>
> **"Why were you searching for me?" he asked. "Didn't you know I had to be in my Father's house?" But they did not understand what he was saying to them. Then he went down to Nazareth with them and was obedient to them. But his mother treasured all these things in her heart. And Jesus grew in wisdom and stature, and in favor with God and men.**
>
> **Luke 2:48-52 NIV**

The wisdom this 12-year-old Boy possessed baffled the godly leaders of Jerusalem. His spiritual wisdom also baffled his parents. At that young age, Jesus was already focused on Kingdom business.

The most important business you can attend to is your Heavenly Father's business, no matter what your age is. This is the hour when children, even those younger than 12, will step forth into Kingdom business as leaders!

When I first started walking with God, everyone told me the things I couldn't do; no one told me the things I *could* do. But there was such a hunger on the inside of me! I still have that hunger for the things of God, and I want God to show up *big*, not small, in my life.

The most important business you can attend to is your Heavenly Father's business, no matter what your age is.

I was taught as a child that God is big, and you have to pay a price to really get to know Him. Salvation is a free gift, but there is more to salvation than being born again and going to Heaven. You must pay a price to get that "something more."

I remember sometimes as a young boy, I'd say to my mother or my grandmother, "I don't want to read the Bible. I think it's boring. I don't want to pray anymore. I think that's boring too."

Mom or Grandma would respond, "That's what you think!" Then they would get after me to pray and read the Bible!

Grandma trained me. A lot of people do not have grandparents or parents to train them as I had, but Grandma was persistent in training me. She helped develop a spiritual hunger in me. If there were more teachers like my grandmother, we would live in a better world. We would be taught how to live in the realm of the Spirit continually — the realm where Christians are supposed to live.

Developing a Spiritual Appetite

It's a sad truth that the glory of God rarely manifests in the lives of many believers. Often the reason people don't flow in the Holy Spirit's timings the way He desires is that they don't truly hunger for the things of God.

You see, a mental desire to see the spectacular is a soulish desire, not spiritual hunger. It will not get you to the place where you will be led by the Holy Spirit, nor will it help you flow with the Holy Spirit. Operating from a mental desire is not being led by the Holy Spirit. You must make yourself "eat" righteousness until your appetite desires more righteousness.

**Often the reason people don't flow
in the Holy Spirit's timings the way He desires
is that they don't truly hunger for the things of God.**

Grandma made me "eat" righteousness. She made me "eat" John 3:16. She made me read my Bible from cover to cover every year that she had charge of me. If I wasn't reading the Word, I was hearing the Word. She continually played cassette tapes of spiritual teaching and preaching.

Television was monitored. Music was monitored. The Word of God prevailed in our home to the point where there was nothing else to see or hear but the things of righteousness. We fellowshipped with people who possessed spiritual hunger, and we weren't allowed to associate with people who didn't desire the things of God.

Our home was like a military academy in some ways. However, divine love flowed freely, causing everything to function properly.

Problems arise when you don't have God's love in the home. Love has the same effect as oil in an engine.

I didn't realize the forces of evil that Grandma kept off me until she finally turned me loose. Once she released me from her protective authority, those forces hit me hard. I thought, *Grandma, let me get back under your control. It's easier there.*

Grandma knew I was having those thoughts, but she said, "No, now you must grow up and be a man."

Grandma operated in great wisdom regarding spiritual training. Now that I am older, I haven't departed from the way of righteousness because she loved me and trained me to hunger and thirst after righteousness, not after the things of the world. The hunger for righteousness got into my blood, and now I desire the things of the Spirit.

Many parents try to do what Grandma did, but they use the power of the rod without the oil of love. Parents like that will likely experience problems with their teenagers. Teenagers often rebel at the things of God when parents provide plenty of discipline to make sure they read the Bible or attend church but don't cultivate loving relationships in their home. Those parents need to ask God to help them express a greater dimension of His love to their children.

Done in love, the rod means correction. Otherwise, spanking is punishment. All of the Bible verses dealing with bringing up children refer to correction or instruction, *not* punishment.

The natural man has a built-in desire for truth and reality. We are created that way. Most of the time, however, we are "programmed" by the world's thinking and the world's system into accepting a counterfeit. What the world labels as truth and reality is usually the very opposite.

Because of Grandma's correction and instruction, I enjoyed the Bible by the time she placed me on my own. I enjoyed hearing about the deep things of God. I hungered for the things of the Spirit. She had fed my natural desire for truth and kept me from the world's counterfeit.

Many parents say, "What is wrong with our children? We've trained them, but somewhere something went wrong."

You cannot say you have trained your children well if you've been setting a wrong example in front of them. You cannot simply *tell* your children what to do. You must *show* them by example.

Much of Grandma's instruction found a home in me because she showed me the truths she taught by the way she led her life.

HUNGER FOR MORE OF HIM

It is time for the Body of Christ to wake up and walk in God's truth. Too many Christians are playing games with God, not hungering or thirsting for His righteousness. Then parents wonder why their children throw off their training and follow a different path when they are older.

I saw people in Africa die because they were physically hungry. But even those Africans who were not starving had a hunger for sweets because they have little of that sort of food. We took candy into Mozambique to give to the children. Some of them had never seen a piece of candy, but once they heard about it or tasted it, they developed a hunger for it. They wanted it!

The man who took us into the little village in Mozambique warned us, "Be careful with that candy because the children will jump you for it."

Not heeding the man's words of wisdom, I pulled the bag of candy out of my pocket and asked the children, "Do you want a piece?"

There were only three pieces of candy in my hand, but they knew I had more. The children could not understand a word I said, but one of the people with me yelled, "Roberts, be careful!"

I thought, *What can these little kids do to me?*

Holding my hand down to the children, I looked at the candy to see how fast it would go — but I did not know my fingers would go with it! They began hitting my hand and pulling on my fingers for more. Those children hungered after that candy! They wanted it!

I began to pray, *Lord, help me get loose from these children!* Finally, I managed to get back in the truck, close the door, and have someone join me on the other side of the seat. I told my companion, "Here is the bag of candy. Count to three, grab as much as you can, and let's throw it out the door." So that's what we did — and we stayed safe!

Our hunger for God and His ways should be far greater than those children's hunger for sweets. We should enjoy what we have now in God, but we should constantly be hungering for more of Him. If we *don't* hunger after the things of God with undying fervency, then when the Holy Spirit shows us His timings and His ways, we won't discern what He is saying to us.

That's why people are missing the moves of God that are happening in their midst right now. Not hungering or thirsting for the things of God makes it easy to miss what the Spirit of God is doing.

If we *don't* hunger after the things of God with undying fervency, then when the Holy Spirit shows us His timings and His ways, we won't discern what He is saying to us.

We must continually want more of God, His presence, His glory, and His power. We must want to talk with Him as our closest Friend. We must want more of Him in every part of our lives!

There came a day when Grandma said, "I've taken you as far as I can. Now it's up to you." She was firm and determined with me, so the only thing I knew to do was what she did — press in to receive more of the things of God.

I would walk the floor, saying, "I want more of You, God. Holy Spirit, flow through me, lead me, teach me, and guide me. I want more of You. I want all I can get, and then I want some more."

How long do you have to walk the floor and say that until you start desiring the things of God? Sometimes it takes months. Set your mind on the things of God. Make your mouth declare your hunger for God. He will answer you when He sees that you mean business with Him.

I made myself do this. I didn't want to at first, but I did it anyway. I spoke these things until I developed a hunger for God. Now I have more of God. I have Him all over me, in me, out of me, and around me!

Set your mind on the things of God.
Make your mouth declare your hunger for God.
He will answer you when He sees
that you mean business with Him.

As I walked the floor in prayer, I was developing my inner man — my spirit man.

By the Holy Spirit in my spirit, I began calling those things that were not as though they were (*see* Rom. 4:17) — and in my pursuit, I received more of God. The gifts of the Holy Spirit began to flow through me. I began to see visions. My spiritual hunger continually increased, and to this day, I still want more of God.

A HUNGER FOR RIGHTEOUSNESS

When I was in Africa, I wanted an American hamburger so badly I could almost see a McDonald's restaurant. I enjoyed and ate African food, but I was hungry for a hamburger. When I arrived back in the United States at the Tulsa International Airport, I didn't say, "Hello," or "It's good to see you" to the people picking me up. I asked, "Where's a McDonald's? I want a hamburger, and I want it now!" A specific, strong *hunger* had developed in me that nothing else could satisfy. I bought a McDonald's hamburger, devoured it, and went back for another one!

There are all kinds of hunger, but there is one hunger that God *requires* us to have — *a hunger for righteousness*.

> **Blessed are they which do hunger and thirst after righteousness: for they shall be filled.**
>
> **Matthew 5:6**

How long do you have to hunger like this before God answers you? <u>Until there is a *proven* hunger.</u>

Some folks satisfy their hunger with the false. Other people give up too easily.

I could have given up on my hunger for a hamburger while I traveled through Africa, but I held on to it. I knew that hamburger was out there somewhere. I got to the point that I was almost willing to take a morning flight to the nearest city that had a McDonald's restaurant so I could eat a hamburger and fly back!

Do you understand that kind of hunger? As silly as it sounds now, I would probably have given 100 dollars for a hamburger that cost only a dollar or two. I *really* wanted one.

To stay spiritually filled and experience spiritual growth, you must continually hunger after the things of God with a far greater intensity than I ever had for that hamburger. Grandma developed that kind of spiritual hunger in me. After I was on my own, I continued to develop that hunger until I became *starved* for more of God.

SPIRITUAL HUNGER CAN BE SATISFIED, BUT ONLY TO HUNGER FOR MORE

After you attain your goal of drawing close to God and begin receiving from Him in times of close communion, your spiritual hunger will always keep reaching for more.

I believe my ministry exploded early on because from about nine years of age on, I was saying, "I want more of God. I hunger after God. I am thirsty for God's living water. I am thirsty for God's knowledge. I am hungry for the things of God."

I have tried to imagine what the next move of His Spirit will be like. What will happen to people when the glory hits? How will I react? The glory is just now beginning to hit a little here and there. Although some churches have struggled through these challenging times, others are beginning to explode with growth.

The Bible promises that you will be filled, yet your hunger for more of God will never come to an end — it goes on forever. To go to the next realm of glory, you must be filled with the level of glory where you are.

Many people get saved and baptized in the Holy Spirit, believe in healing, know that the Word works, and are basically happy with their Christian lives. But they stay on the same level of glory, which always results in spiritual bloating, not spiritual growth. They're not looking for a new realm of glory because they are content where they're at.

But while you are feasting in one realm of glory, your spiritual eyes should always be looking for the next. That is the way to flow with the timings and the ways of God's Spirit.

True spiritual hunger will cause you to devour the Word of God and go back for more. Spiritual hunger causes you to recognize both the genuine and the counterfeit spiritual food. Spiritual hunger will cause the things of the natural realm to become less significant in your life.

While you are feasting in one realm of glory, your spiritual eyes should always be looking for the next. That is the way to flow with the timings and the ways of God's Spirit.

HUNGER ONLY AFTER HIM

Totalitarian governments know that if the people are hungry, they will be easy to rule. Once the authorities provide food, the starving people will do anything their rulers want them to say and think whatever their rulers want them to think. A starving people can be the most militant, mean, and successful force on the earth.

If we desire the things of God, we must be very determined, focused, and even militant in obtaining them. That means we will do whatever is necessary to break down the doors of darkness to receive the true light.

Starving people are often violent people. If we are not "violent" where spiritual food is concerned, we are not truly hungry. I believe this kind of spiritual hunger was what Jesus had in mind when He said: "And from the days of John the Baptist until now the kingdom of heaven suffereth violence, and the violent take it by force" (Matt. 11:12).

If you're a teenager or a young adult, pay close attention to this principle. Make the determined decision early on that you will seek God with all your heart all the days of your life and that with His help and guidance, you won't go down even one detour that takes you away from His good plan for your life. This is the time in your life to begin to walk the floor, deliberately confessing and meditating on God's Word, even if it seems strange to you at first. *Set* your mind on things above (*see* Col. 3:2). Allow the Holy Spirit to plant visions in your heart of the plans God has for you.

Throughout the years ever since when I was a young teenager, I have meditated on the outreaches and missionary work of Roberts Liardon Ministries and on my traveling ministry. I would *see* myself enlarging my circles all the time. I would *see* myself overseas preaching to the masses. I would *see* myself building up the people. I meditated and *meditated* on the dreams God placed in my heart until these things began to come to pass. Yet even today, I am still hungering for more.

Psalm 42:7 says, "Deep calleth unto deep...." If there is a "deep" in you calling, there must be a corresponding "deep" in God to answer the call. If there is a hunger in you, there must be something in Him to satisfy that hunger. If you are hungering for more power, there must be power in Him to receive. If you

are hungering for more love, there must be more of His love to receive.

The late evangelist William Branham told the story of a little boy who ate things containing sulfur. Once he even ate his bicycle pedal — now, that sounds extreme! His parents took him to the doctor, who found that the little boy's body craved sulfur so much that he ate things containing it, not knowing why, nor even knowing those things contained sulfur.

If there is a "deep" in you calling, there must be a corresponding "deep" in God to answer the call. If there is a hunger in you, there must be something in Him to satisfy that hunger.

I have seen African pastors hunger for the things of God in a similar manner, and some of them had only one or two pages of the Bible. Yet they were doing all the right things, not knowing they were following principles of God's Word — and as a result, they were being blessed.

That is the way all Christians are supposed to be. We are to hunger after the things of God with all that is within us — and not search or hunger after anything or anyone *but* Him. The Bible says that if we hunger after God, we will be filled (*see* Matt. 5:6). If we hunger after spiritual things, God will make sure we have everything we need in the natural.

God satisfies my every desire. I am happy with the clothes I wear, the money He provides, and the traveling I do. I am happy with the ministry God has given me. I believe the reason

God satisfies my every need is because I hunger after Him more every day.

SPIRITUAL HUNGER BRINGS BLESSINGS

If you want to be blessed in the natural realm, set your eyes on God. Get your hunger off cars, homes, and bank accounts, and get it focused squarely on God.

Now, I am not looking for a large, personal bank account, but if it comes, I am not going to be foolish enough to turn it down. Some people think that being spiritual means rejecting every material blessing. But God says He causes the wealth of the wicked to come into our hands.

A good man leaveth an inheritance to his children's children: and the wealth of the sinner is laid up for the just.

Proverbs 13:22

When wealth comes, I am certainly not going to return it! I will receive it in Jesus' name. As I walk and hunger after the things of God, He gives me everything I need.

I am trying to propel you to a new level of spiritual hunger. Look for God in everything, and pursue Him like you can never have enough of Him!

Maturing in the School of the Holy Spirit

There's a spiritual law in operation once you have cultivated a spiritual hunger, paid a visit to the Father's house, and received His direction for your life. Regardless of your natural age, a time of preparation must take place before the Holy Spirit alerts you that it's time to step into your call.

I have seen people ignore the need for preparation time or abort this special time only to end up on the spiritual trash heap, no good to anyone because they were not spiritually ready to take on their particular assignment.

GOD'S TIMING IS AS IMPORTANT AS HIS CALL

It is not God's intent for anyone to end up defeated because he or she doesn't know how to battle daily the evil elements of the world. I have seen this type of defeat overtake far too many of God's chosen, called, anointed, and commissioned vessels.

Whatever God has called you to do will require both natural and spiritual preparation. Natural preparation without adequate spiritual preparation will not work. There is no shortcut. Spiritual preparation cannot be avoided or skimped on.

Little or no preparation in the spiritual realm sets the stage for a difficult time when you step out to undertake any assignment from on High. You will get discouraged more easily and give up if your spiritual preparation hasn't been adequate. You could ultimately end up accomplishing nothing of eternal value for God.

**Natural preparation without adequate spiritual preparation
will not work. There is no shortcut.
Spiritual preparation cannot be avoided
or skimped on.**

I have seen people go off to Bible school, and after a short time of preparation and training, conclude that they are ready to conquer the entire world! But after this natural preparation in the knowledge of the Word, they need the spiritual preparation in the school of the Holy Spirit — and that is attained only on their knees in prayer.

There is more to preparation than going to Bible school. I do not want to see more young, anointed ministers of the Gospel devastated beyond repair and losing the harvest of souls they were to gather because of entering the ministry ill-timed and spiritually ill-prepared.

LEARN SPIRITUAL THINGS EARLY

Earlier I gave you some insight into how my grandmother trained me as I was growing up. Grandma's first name was Gladoylene. She was an old-time Pentecostal who, as a teenager, attended a church in Akron, Ohio, where "hellfire and brimstone" were preached. Her church taught that you would not go to Heaven unless you were baptized in the Holy Spirit. (Thank the Lord, we have come a long way since that time.)

Young Gladoylene met people in her church who had been a part of the Azusa Street revival — the beginning of modern-day Pentecostalism. The pastor of this church began a 24-hour prayer chain, and Gladoylene volunteered to pray an hour a day as part of this chain.

People in Grandma's day seemed to be more committed than many believers are today. It is difficult to get people to pray three seconds for the church or for anything else! Yet eternal things merit far more importance than natural things. Believers should be spending more time developing their spirit man and their relationship with God than in any natural pursuit.

Gladoylene's father taught her, "Never tell a lie. Once you have given your word, stick to it at any cost." That's a good philosophy for everyone. We need that preached more often from our local church pulpits.

Once you say you will do something, be willing to die to keep your word. Your word is your bond. Don't let it float around with no meaning or commitment attached.

Gladoylene gave her word that she would pray an hour a day as part of Reverend McKinney's prayer chain. She would set her clock for an hour, but after praying for everything she could think of, she found that only ten minutes had passed.

Prayer requires discipline. And just like exercise, you become better with practice.

Grandma told me, "I would not give up because I had committed myself to that hour. I told that man of God that I would pray an hour for his church, so I was going to do it or die." And she thought she *was* going to die! She would pray about everything she knew to pray about, which back then included only her neighbors, the mayor, policemen, prostitutes, and unsaved loved ones. She was involved in her own little world.

Prayer requires discipline. And just like exercise, you become better with practice.

However, young Gladoylene — just a teenager at the time — hungered and thirsted for the things of God, and it was during this time that she developed into a mighty prayer warrior. The moment she hit her knees in prayer, the Holy Spirit came on the scene. That is what we should all be striving for.

TEACHING BY EXAMPLE

Grandma always enforced what Jesus said. I will never forget the day she looked at me when I was a little boy and said, "Whether you are going to be a successful businessman or a minister of the Gospel, you must know how to pray. So let's begin right now."

Grandma didn't even ask me if I wanted to pray; she *made* me pray. She dragged me into a prayer life! The first day, I didn't want to pray. Like any other kid, I wanted to watch television. Thank God that Grandma was persistent.

She said, "Get on your knees." I obeyed. I was very young at the time.

"Throw up your hands and praise God," she told me. I did.

Grandma said, "Repeat after me." Then she led me in my first Holy Spirit prayer — and never said "Amen"! She just started praying on her own.

Kneeling down beside me, Grandma would say, "I don't want you to move from this spot. If you do, when I get through praying, you are going to get it!"

Grandma would pray for hours, both in tongues and in English. She meant business when she prayed! She would pray things like, "God, help our churches to honor the Bible. Fill the preachers with Holy Spirit fire. If they do not honor You, remove them from the pulpits. Get Holy Spirit men in the pulpits, not dead ones!"

We need that kind of praying today. Grandma knew that dead preachers produce dead people. Fiery preachers produce fire in the church, fire for God, and fire for the things of God. Hallelujah! I saw Grandma literally *pray in* revivals.

When Grandma started fighting demons and coming against the forces of darkness in prayer, that's when things would get interesting. My sister and I watched her. I learned a lot by watching her, and your children will learn best by your example as well — by seeing you pray, by seeing you fight the forces of darkness, and by seeing you intercede for others.

I thought everyone prayed like Grandma. It was a shock when I found out that few Christians pray at all. I wondered what was wrong with everyone else's grandmothers. I wondered what was wrong with their homes.

I was trained in spiritual things in my home by my grandmother and my mother. I was not told, "Go to your room, pray, and read the Scriptures by yourself." Grandma showed me how to pray. She took me with her into the realm of the Spirit. She showed me how to fight demonic forces, how to get the bills paid, and how to pray the right people into positions of leadership and the wrong ones out.

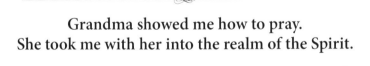

**Grandma showed me how to pray.
She took me with her into the realm of the Spirit.**

You can best show others how to be led by the Spirit of God and flow in the timings of God through the life you live, not by what you say. Talk is cheap, especially in children's eyes. If you are not living what you say you believe, children will not buy what you say.

Grandma always told me, "Don't ever be ashamed of the Gospel. Don't ever be ashamed to yield to the Holy Spirit, wherever you are."

It was normal for Grandma to walk down the aisles in the grocery store praying in tongues. One night God spoke to me in a grocery store and told me to cast the devil out of someone. I flinched a little, but I obeyed. I learned early on that it is best to obey!

When children are trained right, they will not depart from the ways of the Lord when they get old (*see* Prov. 22:6). If you want Holy Spirit-trained children, open your eyes and ears to what He is saying to you about how to train them up in the Lord.

Over the years, I've gotten really tired of seeing children in Christian homes grow up to become messed-up adults. Of course, all must make their own choices to obey God as they grow into adulthood, regardless of others' mistakes. But in most of these cases that I've observed, the parents didn't consistently train their children in the ways of God and model a powerful prayer life before them while they were young.

UNITY AND CORPORATE PRAYER

If any member of Grandma's family faced a situation where he or she couldn't seem to pray through to victory, another family member was called and they prayed in agreement until the battle was won. It is the same in the Body of Christ. When one family member hurts, we all hurt until we pray the situation through to victory.

We've done a lot of that kind of praying in my family. We have agreed together in prayer until everyone's bills were paid. We have stood together until we saw powerful answers to prayer. We have hounded Heaven's doors until God intervened in situations. I believe sometimes God must have said, *"Let's answer their prayers so they will be quiet!"*

Our family knew how to be persistent in prayer, which is one of the keys to a successful prayer life and a walk with God that keeps you in step with the leading and timings of God. Confession of the Word is important, but it must be reinforced with fervent, persistent prayer to be effective.

I am convinced that corporate prayer, unity, and love are God's design for the entire Body of Christ. Only in this manner will we overcome some of the hurdles we face in this day and hour. God is calling us to use power and discernment — both sharpened and honed through prayer in the Spirit. Then everywhere we walk, we will tear up the devil's strategies before they are ever released!

> **But ye, beloved, building up yourselves on your most holy faith, praying in the Holy Ghost, keep yourselves in the love of God, looking for the mercy of our Lord Jesus Christ unto eternal life.**
>
> **Jude 1:20-21**

I believe Grandma knew these verses very well, because when my sister Priscilla and I came home from school, she would take us in a room, shut the door, and say, "Now hit your knees. I want to hear you pray in tongues loud enough for both your ears and mine to hear."

Why did Grandma do that? Although it seemed weird to my sister and me at first, her requirement that we spend time praying in tongues every day strengthened us in our walk with the Lord and in our boldness to stand for Jesus in every situation.

**God is calling us to use power and discernment —
both sharpened and honed through prayer in the Spirit.
Then everywhere we walk, we will tear up
the devil's strategies before they are ever released!**

If we didn't pray loud enough, Grandma would say, "I can't hear you!"

That is how to train your children in the ways of the Lord. Teach them about the realm of the Spirit and about discerning a demon from an angel. In prayer, your children will learn to distinguish the voice of God from a human or demonic voice.

Grandma knew how to raise children, and she knew how to build churches. She would head up prayer groups and teach them exactly as she taught us. She would set the example of how to pray, and she would correct in love when someone got in the flesh. As a result, the power of the Holy Spirit cleaned up both the individuals and the church.

SPIRITUAL TRAINING BEGINS IN THE HOME

I am convinced that God ordained parents to take the lead in the training program I went through with Grandma — not Sunday school teachers, nursery school teachers, or Christian school teachers. The training of a child's spirit must begin in the home.

During my early years when my mom was busy earning her degrees and working to provide for the family, my life consisted mostly of Grandma, God, me, and my bedroom. That is when I learned to pray. The day came when Grandma no longer had to push me into spiritual things, particularly in prayer. I had learned to enjoy praying with great boldness. I desired to pray in the Spirit, and everything else became secondary. I hungered for the things of the Spirit.

The day came when I would say, "Grandma, let's go pray." She would answer, "We haven't had breakfast yet!"

I'd respond, "I don't care. Let's pray, Grandma. Let's go set people free from devils! Let's pray for the man next door."

I would pray as long as I could and get as close to Grandma as I could — because the closer I was to her, the more I'd be in the midst of God's power when it fell. I wanted Grandma to get into that realm. I wanted the glory of God to hit. I enjoyed shaking under the power of God. I knew I'd be strengthened when the glory hit.

The day came when Grandma no longer had to push me into spiritual things, I desired to pray in the Spirit, and everything else became secondary. I hungered for the things of the Spirit.

Before Grandma and I prayed, I'd make sure she was comfortable and had her glass of water, her handkerchief, and her pillows. I'd check to make sure that the phone was off the hook and that no one would be coming to the door. I knew prayer time was a time when we didn't want to be disturbed in any way. No interruptions were allowed.

That was the standard Grandma set within me as a boy that shows me how to treat the prophets of God today. A sigh from Grandma, a move of her little finger, and I knew what that meant. I knew Grandma better than anyone else knew her.

That is the way you should be when a man or woman of God comes across your path. By the Spirit of God, you will know what is needed and what to say.

Grandma would discern through the Holy Spirit when family members had difficulties, even those who lived a great distance away. She would pray, and we would soon see the manifestation of her prayers. Family members in difficulty were soon restored to God.

> **The eyes of the Lord are upon the righteous, and his ears are open unto their cry. The face of the Lord is against them that do evil, to cut off the remembrance of them from the earth. The righteous cry, and the Lord heareth, and delivereth them out of all their troubles.**
>
> **Psalm 34:15-17**

Grandma had a "hotline" to God, and I knew it by the fruit of her labor.

PASSING ON THE FIRE
TO THE NEXT GENERATION

To thrive in these unprecedented times and to continually stay in sync with God's timings, we must stay keenly tuned to the

Holy Spirit. Grandma sharpened my human spirit to hear the Spirit of God as I became her "Elisha."

You need to train your children to be your "Elishas." Elisha knew everything about Elijah. When it was time for Elijah to go home to Heaven, he asked Elisha, "What do you want of me? You have been a great blessing to me. You have helped me fight the battles. You have helped me run the race well. Now, what can I do for you?" (*see* 2 Kings 2:9).

The way Elisha responded to Elijah as the time neared for the elder prophet to leave this earth is revealing. It shows us that Elisha was completely committed to Elijah and to the call of God.

> **And it came to pass, when the Lord would take up Elijah into heaven by a whirlwind, that Elijah went with Elisha from Gilgal. And Elijah said unto Elisha, Tarry here, I pray thee; for the Lord hath sent me to Bethel. And Elisha said unto him, As the Lord liveth, and as thy soul liveth, I will not leave thee. So they went down to Bethel And the sons of the prophets that were at Bethel came forth to Elisha, and said unto him, Knowest thou that the Lord will take away thy master from thy head to day? And he said, Yea, I know it: hold ye your peace. And Elijah said unto him, Elisha, tarry here, I pray thee; for the Lord hath sent me to Jericho.**
>
> **And he said, As the Lord liveth, and as thy soul liveth, I will not leave thee. So they came to Jericho. And the sons of the prophets that were at Jericho came to Elisha, and said unto him, Knowest thou that the Lord will take away thy master from thy head to day? And he answered, Yea, I know it: hold ye your peace. And Elijah said unto him, Tarry, I pray thee, here; for the Lord hath sent me to**

Jordan. And he said, As the Lord liveth, and as thy soul liveth, I will not leave thee. And they two went on.

And fifty men of the sons of the prophets went, and stood to view afar off: and they two stood by Jordan. And Elijah took his mantle, and wrapped it together, and smote the waters, and they were divided hither and thither, so that they two went over on dry ground. And it came to pass, when they were gone over, that Elijah said unto Elisha, Ask what I shall do for thee, before I be taken away from thee. And Elisha said, I pray thee, let a double portion of thy spirit be upon me. And he said, Thou hast asked a hard thing: nevertheless, if thou see me when I am taken from thee, it shall be so unto thee; but if not, it shall not be so.

And it came to pass, as they still went on, and talked, that, behold, there appeared a chariot of fire, and horses of fire, and parted them both asunder; and Elijah went up by a whirlwind into heaven. And Elisha saw it, and he cried, My father, my father, the chariot of Israel, and the horsemen thereof!

And he saw him no more: and he took hold of his own clothes, and rent them in two pieces. He took up also the mantle of Elijah that fell from him, and went back and stood by the bank of Jordan; and he took the mantle of Elijah that fell from him, and smote the waters, and said, Where is the Lord God of Elijah? and when he also had smitten the waters, they parted hither and thither: and Elisha went over. And when the sons of the prophets which were to view at Jericho saw him, they said, The spirit of Elijah doth rest on Elisha. And they came to meet him, and bowed themselves to the ground before him.

2 Kings 2:1-15

Elisha asked for a double portion of the prophet Elijah's spirit. He wanted all that Elijah had and more, and Elisha went on to do many great miracles for God throughout the rest of his life.

This came about as a result of the training Elisha had received from Elijah. There was an essential time of preparation Elisha went through before God could give him Elijah's mantle.

Parents need to put their children through a time of preparation — spirit, soul, and body — similar to the way my Grandma prepared me. But even before that, parents need to develop their own hunger for God. As they consistently live their lives out of that hunger and train their children to continually pursue more of Him, the children will be positioned to catch their parents' fire for God and develop their own desire to pursue Him with all their hearts.

**There was an essential time of preparation
Elisha went through before God
could give him Elijah's mantle.**

We're going after the successful passing of spiritual fire from one generation to the next! That's what happened for Elisha when it was time for him to take the mantle from Elijah and fulfill his own ministry before the Lord.

CHAPTER 8

Sin Squelches
Spiritual Hunger

God wants a glorious Church — one without wrinkle or blemish (*see* Eph. 5:26-27). It's important to realize that the spots, wrinkles, and blemishes that the apostle Paul talked about are the sins of believers, not the sins of *un*believers.

Sin is a killer! It will squelch spiritual hunger and block the flow of the Holy Spirit in your life. In fact, sin unchecked will *halt* the move of the Holy Spirit in your life and pull you out of the timings of God.

In studying the lives of great preachers of the past, I have noticed that many of them lost their power, their crowds, their families, and even their own lives because of sin. Sin destroyed everything they had.

We need to understand that in God's eyes, there is no degree of sin. In today's society, we tend to place degrees on sins, thinking, *This one isn't too bad, but this other one is simply horrible.*

The Bible simply says that the man who avoids the path of sin and embraces the Word of God will be blessed.

> **Blessed is the man that walketh not in the counsel of the ungodly, nor standeth in the way of sinners, nor sitteth in the seat of the scornful. But his delight is in the law of the Lord; and in his law doth he meditate day and night. And he shall be like a tree planted by the rivers of water, that bringeth forth his fruit in his season; his leaf also shall not wither; and whatsoever he doeth shall prosper.**
>
> **Psalm 1:1-3**

THE DESIRE TO LIVE A HOLY LIFE

God's Word has a lot to say about living a holy and righteous life. If you truly hunger after the things of the Spirit of God, you will desire to live a holy life.

> **Blessed is the man who fears the Lord, who delights greatly in His commandments. His descendants will be mighty on earth; the generation of the upright will be blessed. Wealth and riches will be in his house, and his righteousness endures forever.**
>
> **Psalm 112:1-3 NKJV**

> **Blessed are the undefiled in the way, who walk in the law of the Lord! Blessed are those who keep His testimonies, Who seek Him with the whole heart!**
>
> **Psalm 119:1-2 NKJV**

It is God's desire that we be perfect, or blameless, in Him.

Thou shalt be blameless before the Lord thy God.

Deuteronomy 18:13 NKJV

God speaks to us about letting the light of Christ radiate through us.

Let your light so shine before men, that they may see your good works, and glorify your Father which is in heaven.

Matthew 5:16

And they shall call them The Holy People, The Redeemed of the Lord; and you shall be called Sought Out, A City Not Forsaken.

Isaiah 62:12 NKJV

The Kingdom of Heaven is prepared for a holy people.

Do you not know that the unrighteous will not inherit the kingdom of God? Do not be deceived. Neither fornicators, nor idolaters, nor adulterers, nor homosexuals, nor sodomites, nor thieves, nor covetous, nor drunkards, nor revilers, nor extortioners will inherit the kingdom of God. And such were some of you. But you were washed, but you were sanctified, but you were justified in the name of the Lord Jesus and by the Spirit of our God.

1 Corinthians 6:9-11 NKJV

God tells us to be active in avoiding sin.

But he who is joined to the Lord is one spirit with Him. Flee sexual immorality. Every sin that a man does is outside the body, but he who commits sexual immorality sins against his own body. Or do you not know that your body

is the temple of the Holy Spirit who is in you, whom you have from God, and you are not your own? For you were bought at a price; therefore glorify God in your body and in your spirit, which are God's.

1 Corinthians 6:17-20 NKJV

God spoke through Paul, saying, *"Awake to righteousness."* That is a command, not a suggestion!

Awake to righteousness, and sin not; for some have not the knowledge of God: I speak this to your shame.

1 Corinthians 15:34

Paul continued to write on the theme of holy living in his letter to the church at Galatia.

Be not deceived; God is not mocked: for whatsoever a man soweth, that shall he also reap. For he that soweth to his flesh shall of the flesh reap corruption; but he that soweth to the Spirit shall of the Spirit reap life everlasting. And let us not be weary in well doing: for in due season we shall reap, if we faint not.

Galatians 6:7-9

In essence, Paul was saying, "We are not called to filth; we are called to holiness."

For God hath not called us unto uncleanness, but unto holiness.

1 Thessalonians 4:7

The theme of holiness is also discussed by the Apostle Peter:

But as he which hath called you is holy, so be ye holy in all manner of conversation; because it is written, Be ye holy; for I am holy.

1 Peter 1:15-16

Most believers have their outward man well organized to avoid sin. However, internal sins of the soul that aren't dealt with — lust, bitterness, jealousy, and so forth — will kill a person's forward progress in God and eventually possibly even kill *the person* if those sins aren't dealt with.

Therefore do not let sin reign in your mortal body, that you should obey it in its lusts. And do not present your members as instruments of unrighteousness to sin, but present yourselves to God as being alive from the dead, and your members as instruments of righteousness to God. For sin shall not have dominion over you, for you are not under law but under grace.

What then? Shall we sin because we are not under law but under grace? Certainly not! Do you not know that to whom you present yourselves slaves to obey, you are that one's slaves whom you obey, whether of sin leading to death, or of obedience leading to righteousness?

Romans 6:12-16 NKJV

You are the one who chooses whether to live
a life of holiness and righteousness or a life of sin.

In verse 12, Paul's instruction to "let not" sin reign in your body indicates that it is your decision as a believer to sin or not to sin. Those words "let not" have everything to do with your personal will. *You* are the one who chooses whether to live a life of holiness and righteousness or a life of sin.

SIN BEGINS IN THE MIND

The devil cannot *make* you sin. The only thing the devil can do is offer you the *temptation* to sin. He puts the sin before you. However, you are the one who makes the decision, *Am I going to yield to sin or to God?*

> **"You have heard that it was said to those of old, 'You shall not commit adultery.' But I say to you that whoever looks at a woman to lust for her has already committed adultery with her in his heart."**
>
> **Matthew 5:27-28 NKJV**

In these verses, Jesus was speaking of mental sins. The mind must be renewed and transformed by the washing of the Word of God. Only then will we be rid of sinful thoughts and imaginations.

A wandering mind may think an evil thought, such as a thought of adultery. But as believers, we are to *set* our minds on things above and think only on what is true, honest, pure, lovely, and of a good report (*see* Col. 3:2; Phil. 4:8).

Sin will short-circuit God's power operating in your life and block your communication line to His throne room. Yet God's power and the leading of His Spirit are the two essentials you must have to carry out His will *His way* and according to *His time.*

God's glory and sin will simply *never* mix. Shake yourself free from sin completely so you are prepared to taste of God's glory and live. If sin is not dealt with, when God's glory is released, an explosion will take place, resulting in judgment, even death at times (*see* Acts 5:1-11).

Jonathan Edwards, a revivalist preacher during the 18th-century Great Awakening, preached a famous sermon entitled, "Sinners in the Hands of an Angry God." When he would preach this sermon, people would quake and shake with conviction in the middle of the service. But contrary to popular opinion, this sermon was not about the wrath of God; it was about His mercy. Edwards preached about how forbearing God is when our unrighteousness comes into contact with His holiness. Edwards stressed what God has a perfect right to do — but *doesn't* do because He loves us.

We need some of that reverent fear of a holy God restored to our churches today.

The blood of Jesus is not your "insurance policy" that gives you a pass to go out and knowingly commit sin with the intention of asking for forgiveness the next morning. As a child of God, you have the Holy Spirit empowering you from the inside out, making it just as easy to do what is right as it is to sin. But the choice is yours. You must make the decision whether to travel the road of sin or the road of righteousness.

**The blood of Jesus is not your "insurance policy"
that gives you a pass to go out and knowingly commit sin
with the intention of asking for forgiveness
the next morning.**

Until you make the decision to live a life of holiness, your ability to accurately walk out God's plan and flow in His timings will be nonexistent. You see, there are no "big" or "little" sins with God. In His eyes, sin is sin. When you willfully sin, you sow seed that will grow because the devil will make sure it is watered. That sin will bring forth fruit after its kind: corruption and death.

Just as an apple seed produces apples, if you sow sin, you are going to reap sin. And God doesn't cause that seed to grow and produce — *you* do. To cultivate good fruit in your life, you must sow good seeds of righteousness and see that those seeds are watered with the Word.

What about the sin of ignorance? I used to preach a sermon entitled, "Sin No More," in which I would provide people with an escape route. Everyone loved it! I would say, "If you are ignorant, you can plead ignorance before the throne of God, and He will okay it."

Then God showed me that I was wrong about that point. The Spirit of God said to me, *"When Jesus went to Heaven, He sent the Holy Spirit — the great Teacher — back to the earth to guide His people into all truth."*

However, when He, the Spirit of truth, has come, He will guide you into all truth; for He will not speak on His own authority, but whatever He hears He will speak; and He will tell you things to come.

John 16:13 NKJV

We are to be led by the Spirit of God in all we do; therefore, ignorance is not a viable excuse because the Spirit of God will guide us and keep us on the right path.

The truth is, you have *no* legitimate excuse to continue in sin. But don't try not to sin. Simply make a decision not to sin and stick with your decision. Draw on the power of the Holy Spirit within to help you overcome temptation in every situation.

> **Do not be unequally yoked together with unbelievers. For what fellowship has righteousness with lawlessness? And what communion has light with darkness? And what accord has Christ with Belial? Or what part has a believer with an unbeliever? And what agreement has the temple of God with idols? For you are the temple of the living God. As God has said: "I will dwell in them and walk among *them*. I will be their God, and they shall be My people."**

> **Therefore "Come out from among them and be separate, says the Lord. Do not touch what is unclean, and I will receive you. I will be a Father to you, and you shall be My sons and daughters, says the Lord Almighty."**

> **2 Corinthians 6:14-18 NKJV**

When temptation comes, let the devil keep the temptation. How? Step apart from sin. Separate yourself unto a life of godliness.

> The truth is, you have *no* legitimate excuse to continue in sin. But don't try not to sin. Simply make a decision not to sin and stick with your decision.

How To Flow in the Timings of God

Corporate Sin

One of the most prominent corporate sins is gossip. Where corporate sin abounds, corporate judgment will come.

God's army is the only army I know that kills its own wounded. In our natural world, doctors stand by doctors; lawyers stand by lawyers; family members stand by family members. Why can't ministers stand by ministers and believers stand by fellow believers?

King Saul made several attempts to kill David. Yet when Saul died, David wept bitterly.

> **Then David lamented with this lamentation over Saul and over Jonathan his son.... "The beauty of Israel is slain on your high places! How the mighty have fallen! Tell it not in Gath, proclaim it not in the streets of Ashkelon — lest the daughters of the Philistines rejoice, lest the daughters of the uncircumcised triumph."**
>
> **1 Samuel 20:17,20-21 NKJV**

David was saying, "Don't tell the people of other lands that our king is dead. Don't tell them how he died so that they can gloat over his demise. Let's keep it quiet."

That is the way it should be in the Church. Don't publish the failures of other ministers and believers. Make sure your own life is right; then pray for that erring brother or sister. It is a sin not to stand by fellow believers and ministers and support them when they are going through a hard time.

As believers, we are to pour on the oil and the wine and bind up others' wounds. We are to keep the Church glorious. As for our personal walk with the Lord, we are to sin no more.

He has empowered us by His Spirit to live in holiness and do what is right in His eyes. We need to have a reverence toward the awesomeness of God and the magnitude He has wrought in our lives — knowing that from His breath can come destruction or blessing.

As believers, we are to pour on the oil
and the wine and bind up others' wounds.
We are to keep the Church glorious.

Having therefore these promises, dearly beloved, let us cleanse ourselves from all filthiness of the flesh and spirit, perfecting holiness in the fear of God.

2 Corinthians 7:1

As we aim for holiness as a lifestyle, we will grow in our hunger for spiritual things. Only as we step aside from sin and from the temptations of the world will we begin to continually want more of God and learn to flow in His ways and His timings.

Dear friends, now we are children of God, and what we will be has not yet been made known. But we know that when Christ appears, we shall be like him, for we shall see him as he is. All who have this hope in him purify themselves, just as he is pure.

1 John 3:2-3 NIV

Jesus replied, I am the Bread of Life. He who comes to Me will never be hungry, and he who believes in and

cleaves to and trusts in and relies on Me will never thirst any more (at any time).

John 6:35 AMPC

What a blessed assurance Jesus gave us! As we make the decision to lay aside sin and the desires of the flesh and to hunger and thirst for more of God, we will begin to know a walk with Him that is continually filled with His presence.

Part 3

THE PRICE
OF SPIRITUAL HUNGER

Chapter 9

Fit for the Master's Use

In the most agonizing moment of Jesus' life, He cried out, "...Father, if it is Your will, take this cup away from Me; nevertheless not My will, but Yours, be done" (Luke 22:42 NKJV). The *Amplified Bible, Classic Edition* says, "...Father, if You are willing, remove this cup from Me; yet not My will, but [always] Yours be done."

Jesus accepted the Father's will — that the Son of God had to die on the Cross of Calvary. It was the way provided through which all mankind might become part of the family of God.

Jesus found no way out of the Cross experience; no one else could take His place. And He faced His Gethsemane alone. While Jesus was enduring the agony of the horror to come, His disciples fell asleep instead of praying. Peter would later deny that he even knew the Messiah!

Then an angel appeared to Him from heaven, strengthening Him. And being in agony, He prayed more earnestly. Then His sweat became like great drops of blood falling down to the ground. When He rose up from prayer, and had come to His disciples, He found them sleeping from sorrow. Then He said to them, "Why do you sleep? Rise and pray, lest you enter into temptation."

Luke 22:43-46 NKJV

Today you and I must face our own "cross experiences." That cross is different for each person. Our cross experience will correspond to whatever God has asked each of us to do — but what we all have in common is the fact that we must die to self.

To be productive for the Kingdom of God, there is no alternative and no way out of dying to self. Jesus said, "And whoever does not carry their cross and follow me cannot be my disciple" (Luke 14:27 NIV).

To reject your cross experience is literally to play games with God. To reject your cross experience means that you are not really serious about the things of God, and He is not top priority in your life. When you are willing to die to self — to let your flesh die — you become serious about the things of God. *To die to self is to begin to live!*

To be productive for the Kingdom of God, there is no alternative and no way out of dying to self.

There is a price to pay to be fit for the Master's use, to walk in His ways and to flow with His times and His seasons. There is a price to pay for pursuing your spiritual hunger.

Therefore if anyone cleanses himself from the latter, he will be a vessel for honor, sanctified and useful for the Master, prepared for every good work.

2 Timothy 2:21 NKJV

To be acceptable for the Master's use, you must lay aside the weights of anything that would hold you to this earth's realm. You must let your flesh die and learn to yield to Him more and more until you live continually in the realm of the Holy Spirit. *This* is the price of spiritual hunger.

Laying Aside the Weights

Wherefore seeing we also are compassed about with so great a cloud of witnesses, let us lay aside every weight, and the sin which doth so easily beset us, and let us run with patience the race that is set before us, looking unto Jesus the author and finisher of our faith; who for the joy that was set before him endured the cross, despising the shame, and is set down at the right hand of the throne of God.

Hebrews 12:1-2

God is calling to all His sons and daughters in this hour: *"Lay aside every weight and be loosed from anything that binds you to the things of the earth. Be free of everything that would keep you from fulfilling My call or hinder your ability to stay in sync with My Spirit."*

I learned something about this message a long time ago when I was a young boy with a call of God on my life. At that time, no one seemed to care who I was, no one knew I had gone to Heaven, and no one heard my praying grandmother continually declare, "One day Roberts will do something great for the Kingdom of God!"

God is calling to all His sons and daughters in this hour:
*"Be free of everything that would keep you
from fulfilling My call or hinder your ability
to stay in sync with My Spirit."*

For six long years when I was a teenager, I separated myself unto God. I walked my bedroom floor praying in other tongues — sometimes all night long. When I'd go to my room for this special time with the Lord, I would take my Bibles, pads of paper, pencils, and a tape recorder. I wanted to hear from Heaven. I stepped aside from many of the activities of my family, neighborhood, and school. I lay aside all sports to spend this time alone with the Lord.

Many people outside my immediate family thought I was crazy, and they didn't mind telling me so. Not one person seemed to care that I paced the floor with tears streaming down my face because I wanted to hear from God. I wanted nothing but His divine direction for my life.

As I walked my bedroom floor during those six years, I was confronted with evil spirits. But at the same time, I was confronted with glorious angelic hosts from God's realm who sang and ministered to me, strengthening me in my spirit. During this time of separation, I learned the reality of something I'd often heard Kathryn Kuhlman say: "God is not seeking the golden vessels of this earth. He is not seeking the silver vessels. He is seeking the plain, ordinary, yielded vessels who will obey whatever He asks them to do."

When God speaks, we are to heed His voice. We are not to ask questions or hold committee meetings dominated by the intellects of men and women to discuss spiritual matters. When God speaks, we are to obey instantly, knowing that He can be trusted to perform His Word, that He is faithful to keep His promises, that He delights in quickly fulfilling His promises, and that He will never fail us! Anytime God speaks, we can be confident that He will follow through to cause the manifestation of what He has spoken to come forth.

If God says, "Jump through the wall," we are not to ask where the hole is — we are to jump and let Him worry about the hole!

That may sound a little ridiculous, but that is how strong our faith and trust in God should be.

**Anytime God speaks, we can be confident
that He will follow through to cause the manifestation
of what He has spoken to come forth.**

In the following passage of Scripture, we can hear God's voice calling to His people today as He challenges the heathen nations to wake up their mighty men and prepare for war:

Proclaim ye this among the Gentiles; prepare war, wake up the mighty men, let all the men of war draw near; let

them come up: beat your plowshares into swords and your pruning hooks into spears: let the weak say, I am strong. Assemble yourselves, and come, all ye heathen, and gather yourselves together round about: thither cause thy mighty ones to come down, O Lord. Let the heathen be wakened, and come up to the valley of Jehoshaphat: for there will I sit to judge all the heathen round about.

Put ye in the sickle, for the harvest is ripe: come, get you down; for the press is full, the vats overflow; for their wickedness is great. Multitudes, multitudes in the valley of decision: for the day of the Lord is near in the valley of decision.

Joel 3:9-14

God is also saying in *this* hour, *"Wake up the mighty men and women — those who have pure hearts and motives toward Me and who know how to pray in the Spirit until victory comes! Wake up those whom the world has despised and rejected because it traffics in the traditions of men that are contrary to Me."*

In this last outpouring of the Holy Spirit, we will face great battles. We must loose all the chains and weights that have kept us tied to the earth. Then as we learn to flow with the precious Holy Spirit, we will be out ahead of the battles before they hit!

We must be able to go into the very throne room of God, sit around His conference table, and receive our plans and orders directly from Him. We are standing at a crossroads, both as individual believers and as the Church. Every believer and every local church body must shake loose from all entanglements of the world to be able to respond with immediacy to God's end-time directives.

Many people have taken a few steps into the realm of the Spirit to hear from God but have failed to remain there. Because they have not let go of all worldly entanglements, they cannot receive the fullness of God's specific plans designed just for them.

Those who walk in the flesh will discourage you if you attempt to move completely into the realm of the Spirit. They will often say things like, "Be normal. Don't be weird." Have you ever heard that? What they are really saying is, "Be like us!"

What weights or entanglements are bogging you down? Is it sports, food, wrong friendships, television, an apathetic attitude, pride, sickness, or debt? Whether it is one of these areas or something else, get rid of it and step into the liberty wherein Christ has set you free. God's Word provides the way of escape out of every entanglement. Diligently seek God through prayer and His Word so you will be able to flow with His Spirit and in His timings.

Consider yourself a runner in the race Christ has set before you. No runner with even a thimbleful of sense would weigh himself down before entering a race. He would shake free of everything that might hinder his chances to win. He would want that freedom in order to run his very best.

Paul wrote about the race of life. He was referring to dying to the flesh and being free in Christ when he wrote of putting his body under.

Do you not know that those who run in a race all run, but one receives the prize? Run in such a way that you may obtain it. And everyone who competes for the prize is temperate in all things. Now they do it to obtain a perishable

crown, but we for an imperishable crown. Therefore I run thus: not with uncertainty. Thus I fight: not as one who beats the air. But I discipline my body and bring it into subjection, lest, when I have preached to others, I myself should become disqualified.

1 Corinthians 9:24-27 NKJV

No longer can we run with the world and also run with God. No longer can we straddle the fence and serve both God and mammon (*see* Matthew 6:24). We must make a choice. We cannot live for God part of the time and for the devil the rest of the time. We must choose whom we will serve.

Ye cannot drink the cup of the Lord, and the cup of devils: ye cannot be partakers of the Lord's table, and of the table of devils. Do we provoke the Lord to jealousy? are we stronger than he? All things are lawful for me, but all things are not expedient: all things are lawful for me, but all things edify not.

1 Corinthians 10:21-23

The weights of this world must be laid aside quickly. You and I — as well as *all* of God's mighty men and women — must enter the Spirit realm free of encumbrances if we are to be totally effective for God and do mighty exploits for Him.

We must make a choice. We cannot live for God
part of the time and for the devil the rest of the time.
We must choose whom we will serve.

CHAPTER 11

Dying to Self

I used to ride on the coattail of my grandmother's spirit. I knew that whenever she moved into the glory world, those goose bumps would pop up on me as well. I knew that if I stayed close enough to her, she could "piggyback" me into the realm of the Spirit. But one day God said, *"Now it is your fight. Now you will be held accountable for your own spirit."*

When that release came, I began to realize what my grandma had kept me from and the protection she had been to me. Until that time, my mind had never been confused. I had never known what it was to be tormented by evil spirits because she had kept them away from me.

I can remember times when I came home from school as a youngster, and Grandma would abruptly stop me and pray for me before I barely got my nose inside the front door! She could see into the realm of the spirit at times, and she'd when I had demonic spirits hovering over me. Thank God for Grandma!

But the day came when I had to learn to pray and get into the realm of the Spirit for myself. I began to realize that no person or ministry would ever succeed because of a great education, financial success, or connections made by man. These things do not entice the anointing of God to fall upon a person because the Holy Spirit causes the anointing to fall as *He* wills, never as man wills. The Holy Spirit never takes directions from man.

Pay the Price — Persist in Your Pursuit of God

God's anointing comes upon yielded vessels — vessels who totally submit and surrender to the Spirit of God. I had to learn to yield to the Holy Spirit, and as I did, the anointing upon me became stronger.

I have learned that yielding to the Holy Spirit and living in the realm of the Spirit is an ongoing process. As we mature in Christ, we can learn more and more how to yield more fully to the Holy Spirit. *But the only way to make the realm of the Spirit our habitation is to spend much time alone with God.*

During the first year that I walked my bedroom floor praying and weeping before God, I would look out the window and see my friends playing baseball. My flesh would say, *You're not accomplishing a thing! Go play baseball with your friends. You are not even getting a single goose bump, Roberts!* (That is the kind of encouragement I received from my mind.)

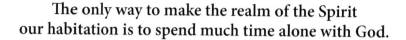

**The only way to make the realm of the Spirit
our habitation is to spend much time alone with God.**

The truth is, I didn't receive even one goose bump for more than a year! I felt nothing. There was absolutely no response from Heaven that I was able to discern for more than a year.

For most people, if they don't hear from Heaven within five minutes, they are ready to give up. Often they quit praying and start confessing the Word, hoping that their many words will bring immediate results.

But confession will not work unless it is enforced with prayer. You can confess the Word until you are blue in the face, but unless your prayer life is up to par, your confession will not avail.

Others get into trouble in this area of seeking God because they are looking for feelings or are seeking the approval of men.

You cannot go by feelings or men's approval. The quality of your time spent with God is not based on goosebumps or feelings. Spending time in prayer develops a spiritual maturity that gives you a spiritual confidence — a supernatural knowing that you are doing something that is producing eternal results.

I knew that if I persisted with God, He would finally show up. My attitude was this: *I am going to walk this bedroom floor until God shows up or I die!*

You need that kind of persistence to get hold of God. At times you need old-time Pentecostal persistence that will cause you to pray all night until Heaven hits earth! Dead, dried-up religion isn't worth a thing. Religion kills the spirit and causes the flesh to prevail.

**Spending time in prayer
develops a spiritual maturity that gives you
a spiritual confidence — a supernatural knowing
that you are doing something
that is producing eternal results.**

Criticism and persecution will come as you begin to separate yourself unto God, but you have to get into the realm of the Spirit where you belong. You have to get under the shadow of the Almighty and stay there. You have to get to the place where you are absolutely confident that the winds of God will overshadow you, carry you, and protect you.

> **No weapon that is formed against thee shall prosper; and every tongue that shall rise against thee in judgment thou shalt condemn. This is the heritage of the servants of the Lord, and their righteousness is of me, saith the Lord.**
>
> **Isaiah 54:17**

When I was a teenager, I talked to God as I walked down the school hallways. I wasn't concerned about what others thought of me. I wasn't concerned about a social life or sports. I wanted more of God, and I didn't care what it cost me to have a relationship with Him.

I have to admit that some of the persecution bothered me at first, because my flesh was not completely dead yet. But I learned not to bow to the opinions of others; I learned to go with God. I knew that He would keep me and take care of me, because I was seeking Him first above all these other things that the world deemed important. God was most important to me.

I wanted more of God, and I didn't care what it cost me to have a relationship with Him.

At times I would pray all night. Some people may say, "Oh, you're just exaggerating." No, that is the way it was for me. I was persistent. After more than a year of praying, I walked into my bedroom one day and felt the presence of God.

When you have walked the floor for that long with absolutely no feelings, you will come to recognize when it is God. You sense the power of His presence.

I went for two or three months longer without any further response from God. I kept knocking on Heaven's door to see if Someone would answer.

One day, when I walked into my bedroom and shut the door, God spoke to me, saying, *"Here I am. Seek no more. I have come to hear from you."* When He said that, the power of God filled my room so intensely that I was thrown across the floor. All that night, I shook under the mighty power of God.

This is the type of spiritual encounter people are hungry for. They are seeking the real because they've had enough of the counterfeit. They are looking for God to show up and say, *"Here I am."*

When God says that, He means, *"I will be with you. I will go beside you. I will strengthen you. I will help you. I will heal through you. I will speak through you. I will bless people through you."*

Not too many people have paid the price to get God to visit them, but He is no respecter of persons. What He did for me, He will do for you.

People try to get a visitation from God through great head knowledge. They try to reach God through money or popularity. But God is not influenced by any of these things. He is simply looking for ordinary, yielded vessels.

You can be that yielded vessel. All it takes is dying to your flesh and learning to walk in the Spirit.

DON'T MOURN THE DEATH OF YOUR FLESH

When God came into my room, we began to walk and talk as friends. I became the student, and He became my Teacher. The old Roberts Liardon began to die. God began to take away the desires of my flesh and the goals I had set for my life.

I was destined for college, sports, and other things I had in mind. However, as I began to yield myself as a vessel to God, He slowly reached in and pulled Roberts out. Many nights, it seemed as if He cut me wide open and never used any painkillers. He just reached in and grabbed something I dearly loved in the flesh or something I wanted to do in the natural.

As my flesh began to die, I felt as if I was dying a thousand deaths. I was being nailed to my own cross that I had submitted myself to, and now God was operating on me. He was taking things out of me that were hindering me from fulfilling His call for my life. It took awhile for all those things to be pulled out of me.

One day God took me to what I call a "spiritual graveyard." Every person who means business with God must visit this place — a graveyard where the flesh is buried. I saw a coffin with several angels standing around it. As I walked closer, I looked inside and there lay Roberts Liardon.

As I saw myself in that coffin, I began to cry. There lay my wife, my children, my college, my basketball career — everything I had ever wanted or planned for my life. And I was the only one who had the power to shut the coffin.

Until that day, I hadn't known what it really meant to "see self die." I hadn't understood the reality of seeing self fight for survival. I had never realized how powerful self was. I didn't realize at that point in my life that the most exciting and beautiful life possible cannot begin until self dies.

After I shut the lid of my coffin that day, I was buried. Then I wrote on my tombstone: *"Here lie the remains of Kenneth Roberts Liardon."*

When I left the "graveyard," I was sad. It is quite a task to bury your own self, your own desires. I believe it is the hardest thing Christians must do while on the earth, surpassing all other spiritual experiences.

When I walked away from that spiritual graveyard that day, I had died. Later I returned to mourn my death, and a huge angel stood in front of the graveyard and said, "Those who mourn the death of self in this place will never be able to be used for the glory of God."

Once self dies and is buried, leave it there! Do not mourn the death of your flesh. Mourning your death will cause self to revive, and it will be harder for you to die to self the second time. The complete death of one's natural self — the carnal desires, thoughts, and behavior — will lead to the resurrection by the Holy Spirit of a Spirit-controlled soul.

Once self dies and is buried, leave it there! Do not mourn the death of your flesh.

Crucifying Self in Order To Live

Never go back to the flesh or the realm of self. Begin living unto God, and you can begin living in the realm of the Spirit on a continual basis.

Put to death, therefore, whatever belongs to your earthly nature: sexual immorality, impurity, lust, evil desires and greed, which is idolatry. Because of these, the wrath of God is coming. You used to walk in these ways, in the life you once lived. But now you must also rid yourselves of all such things as these: anger, rage, malice, slander, and filthy language from your lips. Do not lie to each other, since you have taken off your old self with

its practices and have put on the new self, which is being renewed in knowledge in the image of its Creator.

Colossians 3:5-10 NIV

The first step in living in the realm of the Holy Spirit is to die to yourself. Until you do, God will never be able to use you in the manner He desires. You cannot partially die to self and become alive unto God. You must get to the point where none of self and all of God Almighty remains in you. You must come to the place where you can say with the apostle Paul:

I am crucified with Christ: nevertheless I live; yet not I, but Christ liveth in me: and the life which I now live in the flesh I live by the faith of the Son of God, who loved me, and gave himself for me.

Galatians 2:20

We are not to be ruled by the flesh; we are to be ruled by the Holy Spirit.

So then, brethren, we are debtors, but not to the flesh [we are not obligated to our carnal nature], to live [a life ruled by the standards set up by the dictates] of the flesh.

Romans 8:12 AMPC

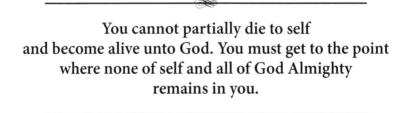

You cannot partially die to self
and become alive unto God. You must get to the point
where none of self and all of God Almighty
remains in you.

The flesh didn't cause the new birth or bring Christ to the earth. The Spirit of God brought Christ to the earth. The Spirit of God raised Jesus from the dead, and that same Holy Spirit lives in you. Now it's up to you to choose to yield yourself to Him.

Many believers yield themselves to the flesh rather than the Holy Spirit and then ask, "Why are my words powerless when I stand to preach? Why doesn't anything happen when I witness to people about Jesus Christ?"

When I tell people of the necessity to die to self and to yield that self to the Holy Spirit, they often laugh, mock, criticize, and persecute. They don't seem to realize that this is the very truth that will set them free.

I believe that if the glory of God came into some churches and homes, His presence would cause the physical deaths of some people because the presence of God will not mix with willful, rebellious sin. In that environment, His presence causes a reaction — an explosion called "judgment and death."

Do you remember what happened to Ananias and Sapphira in the book of Acts? It was not the presence of the apostles that caused them to fall dead when they sinned. No, they fell dead instantly when they lied in the presence of the Holy Spirit. They consciously sinned in the presence of God's glory. Willful sin and God's glory never mix.

Although Peter gave Ananias and Sapphira the choice to repent, they chose to commit spiritual suicide. If the glory of God came in the magnitude and power that some Christians pray for it, many more would also die. God is not a murderer, but He also doesn't diminish the power of His presence to accommodate willful, rebellious sin. He expects His people to live in the light of what they know.

Until you die to self, you cannot live unto righteousness.

For if you live according to [the dictates of] the flesh you will surely die. But if through the power of the [Holy] Spirit you are habitually putting to death (making extinct, deadening) the [evil] deeds prompted by the body, you shall (really and genuinely) live forever.

Romans 8:13 AMPC

Every person is faced with the choice of keeping the flesh alive or dying to self.

People who mean business with God want His presence without limitation or boundaries, but many are not willing to pay the price to get it. They don't want to go through what I'm talking about.

You are responsible for paying a price to step into the fullness of God's presence and to walk in His will and His timings for your life. Your grandma cannot pay the price for you. Your mom, dad, brothers, sisters, aunts, uncles, or cousins cannot pay the price for you. Your pastor cannot pay the price for you. You must die on your own cross and then yield to the Holy Spirit's work in you as He raises you to new life.

Every person is faced with the choice of keeping the flesh alive or dying to self.

I will admit it is a lonely road to that personal cross of dying to self. It is a lonely death on that tree, and it is a lonely funeral. But the glory of the death and burial of self will cause a resurrection to new life! That resurrection is what multitudes of people are looking for today. The key is this: *The only way you can live by the Spirit is to first crucify your flesh.*

Esther's Cross Experience

Esther faced a "cross" experience when she had to choose whether or not to risk her life for the preservation of her people, the Jews, when they lived in exile. No one could approach the king unless he summoned them. Esther made the choice to risk her life and stand in the gap for her people. If the king didn't hold out his golden scepter to her as she approached, the law stated that she must die.

> **And Mordecai told him all that had happened to him, and the sum of money that Haman had promised to pay into the king's treasuries to destroy the Jews. He also gave him a copy of the written decree for their destruction, which was given at Shushan, that he might show it to Esther and explain it to her, and that he might command her to go in to the king to make supplication to him and plead before him for her people. So Hathach returned and told Esther the words of Mordecai.**

> **Then Esther spoke to Hathach, and gave him a command for Mordecai: "All the king's servants and the people of the king's provinces know that any man or woman who goes into the inner court to the king, who has not been called, he has but one law: put all to death, except the one to whom the king holds out the golden scepter, that he may**

live. Yet I myself have not been called to go in to the king these thirty days." So they told Mordecai Esther's words.

And Mordecai told them to answer Esther: "Do not think in your heart that you will escape in the king's palace any more than all the other Jews. For if you remain completely silent at this time, relief and deliverance will arise for the Jews from another place, but you and your father's house will perish. Yet who knows whether you have come to the kingdom for such a time as this?"

Then Esther told them to reply to Mordecai: "Go, gather all the Jews who are present in Shushan, and fast for me; neither eat nor drink for three days, night or day. My maids and I will fast likewise. And so I will go to the king, which is against the law; and if I perish, I perish!" So Mordecai went his way and did according to all that Esther commanded him.

Esther 4:7-17 NKJV

Esther obtained favor in the sight of the king. And because of her willingness to jeopardize her own life — to lay aside what the natural realm seemed to dictate and her flesh's desire to preserve her own life — a great victory was obtained for her people (*see* Esther 8).

Dying to self means obeying God at any cost. Esther did that. Is your flesh dead enough that you would risk your life to save others?

**Dying to self means
obeying God at any cost.**

DANIEL'S CROSS EXPERIENCE

No fault could be found in Daniel. He had an excellent spirit. Daniel didn't bow to the flesh or to what the natural realm would dictate.

> **It pleased Darius to set over the kingdom one hundred and twenty satraps, to be over the whole kingdom; and over these, three governors, of whom Daniel was one, that the satraps might give account to them, so that the king would suffer no loss. Then this Daniel distinguished himself above the governors and satraps, because an excellent spirit was in him; and the king gave thought to setting him over the whole realm.**
>
> **So the governors and satraps sought to find some charge against Daniel concerning the kingdom; but they could find no charge or fault, because he was faithful; nor was there any error or fault found in him.**
>
> **Daniel 6:1-4 NKJV**

Like I said earlier, when a person follows after God, there will be those who are quick to criticize and persecute him or her. Daniel was no different, and his enemies at court knew that they could find no fault in him unless they could set up a situation in which he would have to choose between disobeying the law of his God or the law of the king.

Knowing Daniel would not disobey his God, the dignitaries of the king prepared a decree for King Darius to sign that prohibited any person from praying to any man or god for 30 days. Their petitions were to be routed only to King Darius. The king signed the decree stating that any person who violated the decree was to be cast into the den of lions to be devoured.

All the governors of the kingdom, the administrators and satraps, the counselors and advisors, have consulted together to establish a royal statute and to make a firm decree, that whoever petitions any god or man for thirty days, except you, O king, shall be cast into the den of lions. Now, O king, establish the decree and sign the writing, so that it cannot be changed, according to the law of the Medes and Persians, which does not alter." Therefore King Darius signed the written decree.

Now when Daniel knew that the writing was signed, he went home. And in his upper room, with his windows open toward Jerusalem, he knelt down on his knees three times that day, and prayed and gave thanks before his God, as was his custom since early days. Then these men assembled and found Daniel praying and making supplication before his God.

Daniel 6:7-11 NKJV

His enemies intended the decree to be a weapon against Daniel, a covenant servant of God. God made a way of escape for His own, but before deliverance came, Daniel had to make a choice not to cater to his flesh. He knew his God, and his God knew him. Daniel knew that God's laws are higher than man's laws. He knew he could not compromise and bow to human decree when it came against God's law. Daniel took his stand. He faced his cross. He would not bow.

Daniel was cast into the den of lions for violating the decree, but because he honored God and would not bow to man, he emerged unharmed the next day. Daniel said to the king:

My God sent His angel and shut the lions' mouths, so that they have not hurt me, because I was found innocent before Him; and also, O king, I have done no wrong before

you." Now the king was exceedingly glad for him, and commanded that they should take Daniel up out of the den. So Daniel was taken up out of the den, and no injury whatever was found on him, because he believed in his God.

Daniel 6:22-23 NKJV

When you will not bow to the flesh, to the natural realm, or to man's decrees when they violate God's laws, great strides are made for the Kingdom of God and great glory is given unto God.

> Then King Darius wrote: To all peoples, nations, and languages that dwell in all the earth: Peace be multiplied to you. I make a decree that in every dominion of my kingdom men must tremble and fear before the God of Daniel. For He is the living God, and steadfast forever; His kingdom is the one which shall not be destroyed, and His dominion shall endure to the end.

Daniel 6:25-26 NKJV

Daniel knew he could not compromise and bow
to human decree when it came against God's law.
Daniel took his stand. He faced his cross.
He would not bow.

As you examine the lives of both Old Testament prophets and New Testament figures, you will find that those who remained steadfast — not compromising God's laws and not bowing to the flesh nor to the dictates of the natural realm — achieved great accomplishments for the Kingdom of God. Men and women have always come through challenges as heroes when they refused to disobey God, even at the risk of losing their own lives.

Are you willing to pay that kind of price to serve God? If not, then your flesh needs to die some more! The resurrection power of God will not flow through your life and you will not flow in His times and His seasons until there is death to self.

Men and women have always come through challenges as heroes when they refused to disobey God, even at the risk of losing their own lives.

Chapter 12

Living in the
Realm of the Spirit

The spirit world is an unknown realm to many Christians. Others live every day of their lives there, and they are more conscious of the realm of the Spirit than of the place called earth. Those who operate in the flesh don't understand. They call those who have paid the price to live in the unseen realm "weird," "fanatic," or "in error."

However, the critics cannot outdo the miracles of those who live in the realm of the Spirit. Neither can the critics produce a more anointed sermon than the messages those who live in the Spirit preach!

Romans 8:14-17 (NKJV) reveals that this life in the Spirit requires the flesh to go through some suffering:

For as many as are led by the Spirit of God, these are sons of God. For you did not receive the spirit of bondage again to fear, but you received the Spirit of adoption by whom we cry out, "Abba, Father." The Spirit Himself bears witness with our spirit that we are children of God, and if children, then heirs — heirs of God and joint heirs with Christ, if indeed we suffer with Him, that we may also be glorified together.

I once attended an overseas pastors' conference where I heard nice words spoken. The ministers there acted very friendly. They seemed glad I was there, although I knew some of them wanted money from me and others coveted the same kind of anointing I have. As I glanced around the room, it became obvious which pastors were in the process of dying to self, the ones who had already died to self, and those who were very much still alive to themselves.

The churches pastored by those who had died to self were flourishing — exploding with growth and power and experiencing a great outpouring of God's Spirit. The words of these pastors carried weight. When they walked into a room or down a hallway, they commanded an unconscious respect from those around them.

Then I looked at some of those who had not died to themselves and discerned their thoughts of criticism. The Spirit of God spoke in this meeting, but by a vote of men's minds (the flesh, or soul), they delayed acting in obedience to Him. The Holy Spirit then spoke to me, *"Shake the dust from your shoes. Leave them to themselves, for I am now through with them."*

THE CHURCH IS AT A CROSSROADS

I believe the Body of Christ is standing at a crossroads in this hour. If we don't make a decision to obey the word of the Lord, tomorrow may be too late.

This age is coming to a divine conclusion, and when it closes, where will you be standing? Will you be standing in the flesh? Will you be standing in the midst of your own crumbling world, crying and attempting to put it back together? Will you be found searching for gold, silver, and the riches of this world? Where will you be in your relationship with God?

Here is what you must determine as you stand at this crossroads: *Am I serious about the Kingdom of God? Do I want to be friends with God? Do I want Him to walk and talk with me everywhere I go? Am I willing to pay the price to have that kind of intimate relationship with God?*

I believe the Body of Christ is standing at a crossroads in this hour. If we don't make a decision to obey the word of the Lord, tomorrow may be too late.

If your answer is yes to those questions, you must pick up your own cross and nail your flesh to that tree. You must go to that graveyard and bury your flesh. You must close your coffin, even though your flesh screams for survival. You must help the angels put the soil on top of your coffin.

You must write your own epitaph and shake the dust from your feet as you walk away from your grave. Then you must depart from that graveyard with your head held high and your shoulders back, ready to face a dying humanity.

People who change the course of history have died to self. They don't minister only as human bodies of flesh. They minister as yielded vessels through whom the Lord Jesus Christ Himself speaks, delivers, and heals.

You may be dead to self, but you are alive with the presence of God within you. When you walk out onto a platform to minister, or when you walk into a place of business, you do not walk in as yourself but as a representative of Jesus Christ, the King of Kings and Lord of Lords.

No one can look on a person who has died to self and come alive unto God without coming into contact with the truth of the Gospel. When people have died to self and Jesus walks and talks through them, they act right, speak right, and look right. Because they have made it their way of life to stay in tune with the Holy Spirit, they continually find themselves at the right place at the right time.

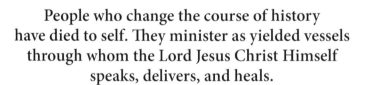

People who change the course of history have died to self. They minister as yielded vessels through whom the Lord Jesus Christ Himself speaks, delivers, and heals.

When someone like that walks into a room, other people will comment, "There is something different about you." This is the kind of person the world is searching for.

The late Kathryn Kuhlman, one of the world's greatest evangelists, said that when she was backstage getting ready to go out before the people, she would die a thousand deaths. She'd say, "I know better than anyone else that Kathryn Kuhlman has nothing to do with what happens here today. It is not me. I have no healing power. I have no saving power. It is not my touch that will do it; it is His touch."

The world needs to see a Christian who is absolutely dead to self so that Jesus shines through. Criticism cannot hurt a dead person. Someone can walk up to a person whose flesh is dead and hit him, and he won't default to a fleshly reaction. This is the kind of person God can use.

Jesus died to self before He died on the Cross so that God could use Him. We must also die to self so God can use *us*.

When I walk down a prayer line and see the hurting, the sick, and the possessed, I know my hands cannot heal them or set them free. I have no power in myself, and neither do you. But when we live as yielded vessels, the power of the Holy Spirit will freely flow through us to heal the sick, bind up the brokenhearted, and set the captives free (*see* Luke 4:18).

Your worldly achievements don't impress God, but your yieldedness does. The secret of understanding the Holy Spirit and allowing Him to flow in your life is yielding yourself to Him. It is not half of you and half of the Holy Spirit. The Holy Spirit doesn't take orders from man or do things when and how man wants it done. He doesn't work with formulas. He gives the orders, and you obey. As you yield yourself completely to Him, He will flow through you.

**The secret of understanding the Holy Spirit
and allowing Him to flow in your life
is yielding yourself to Him.**

Yielded and Obedient —
The Example of God's Generals

I teach a course called "God's Generals" to Bible school students, which includes a discussion of the successes and failures of famous preachers of the past. I go through their lives in great detail, and students always ask, "What caused these men and women to have such a great anointing?"

How could Smith Wigglesworth kick a crippled child from the stage into the congregation in Bradford, England, while the parents and the congregation looked on, paralyzed with fear and anxiety — only for the child to land on both feet, made totally whole by the power of God? God works in unusual ways. At times His ways may seem strange, but the Bible actually says that God's ways *are* strange sometimes!

For example, we read the response of the people when the palsied man was let down through a hole in the roof by his friends and Jesus healed him.

> **And they were all amazed, and they glorified God and were filled with fear, saying, "We have seen strange things today!"**
>
> **Luke 5:26 NKJV**

When the supernatural power of God is allowed to flow freely through an obedient, faithful believer, we will often see strange occurrences!

Charles G. Finney was perhaps the greatest revivalist since the days of the Apostle Paul. A very high percentage of his converts remained true to God. When Finney's horse and buggy came within two or three miles of a town, the convicting power of the Holy Spirit would hit the entire town. Revival hit the place even before Finney reached the outskirts!

Aimee Semple McPherson built a massive building she called Angelus Temple in Los Angeles at a cost of millions of dollars during the Great Depression. She preached 21 times a week. Everywhere she went, people packed the buildings and many had to be turned away. Her name was featured at least six times a week on the front page of the *Los Angeles Times*. She was the first woman to have a Christian radio station.

When Sister McPherson went into a town, she would take it for God. She didn't pray long prayers or preach long sermons, but when she walked out onto the stage to preach, the power of God fell. People were healed as she preached the Word.

Aimee would have what she called "stretcher days." She would announce over her radio station that all who wanted to leave their stretchers should come to Angelus Temple on such and such a day. She would add, "You don't have to be saved. Just come, and you'll get healed. Then you'll want to get saved." She would preach a short sermon, then say, "It is time for you to get up off your stretchers." People got up as she spoke, healed by the power of God.

A man who had no eyeballs, just empty eye sockets, went to one of Sister McPherson's meetings. She prayed for him, and a creative miracle occurred. God created two brand-new eyeballs in the empty sockets!

When you relate these miracles to Bible school students, they want to know how they can have that same kind of power. *That power is available to anyone who will pay the price to receive it.* These individuals we call God's generals weren't special. They were ordinary people who had so completely died to self that Christ could live in and through them, bringing great glory to God. They were simply yielded vessels operating in the power of the Holy Spirit.

And these men and women of God weren't gold or silver vessels. Gold and silver vessels only want to go to men in high places. Gold and silver vessels want some of the attention, glamour, and glory; however, they usually have little or no power. All they are is a shell of what they pretend to be.

These individuals we call God's generals weren't special. They were ordinary people who had so completely died to self that Christ could live in and through them, bringing great glory to God.

God looks for those who have given up all of self. He looks for those who will yield themselves entirely to Him so He can work through them as He wills. I believe that when this type of yieldedness happens in the Church as a whole, we will begin to see the greatest outpouring of the Holy Spirit ever witnessed.

SELFISHNESS GIVES OFF A STENCH

I never realized the importance of what happened to me when my flesh was crucified until I began traveling across the earth.

In the spirit realm, I sometimes notice a stench about some believers and Christian leaders. It is a stench that comes from people who have not died to themselves. They are the ones who are not concerned about lifting up Jesus. Instead, they are thinking, *What about me? Where do I fit in? What is in this for me? If I can't be in the limelight, I don't want to be a part of it.*

That attitude is a stench to God! The odor comes from a disease called selfishness. If you are fighting symptoms of this disease, repent quickly. Humble yourself before God. Refuse to let the spotlight be on anyone except Jesus Christ.

You may say, "Yes, but I have such-and-such talent and ability that I need to use for His Kingdom." You're right. God has placed within you every talent and ability you possess, and all your giftings should be used for His Kingdom — but only to bring glory and honor to Jesus, not to yourself.

Do an attitude check on yourself regularly. Make sure that in everything you do and say, you do it as unto the Lord and not as unto yourself or unto men (*see* Col. 3:17,23). This is how you will see the Holy Spirit's power manifested in your life.

The Bible gives us clear guidelines about what our focus and motivation should be:

Humble yourselves in the sight of the Lord, and he shall lift you up.

James 4:10

And whosoever shall exalt himself shall be abased; and he that shall humble himself shall be exalted.

Matthew 23:12

God will not move with His power and with a manifestation of His presence until we have given up all the things that have held us in bondage. The price each of us must pay will be different, but there will be some similarities.

Too many Christians today want a fast-flying healing evangelist who can get them healed in five minutes. They want the pastor to carry the entire church into the glory of God. They want to ride with God, but they do not want to pay the fare.

Where are the Kathryn Kuhlmans, the Aimee McPhersons, the Smith Wiggleworths, the John G. Lakes, the E. W. Kenyons, the George Jeffreyses, the Martin Luthers, the John Wesleys, the George Whitefields, and the John Alexander Dowies of today? God wants people who are "sold out" to Him to work for the Kingdom. God goes to and fro throughout the whole earth looking for them, and He desires to show Himself strong on their behalf (*see* 2 Chron. 16:9).

Many Bible school students have heard me preach this sermon, only to let it go in one ear and out the other. Some leave school, go into the ministry, and come back demolished a few months later because they have not crucified their flesh.

I am doing my best to help you understand the importance of nailing yourself to your cross. For you to fulfill your part in

God's great plan according to His ways and His timings, it is absolutely critical that you die to self. You must continually cry out to God with your whole heart, *"Not my will, but Thy will be done."*

This is the crossroads where the Church stands today.

Let the weights of this world fall away, including those friends who don't desire the things of the Kingdom of God. As for you, pursue Jesus above all. Do not seek the spectacular. Seek *Him.*

**You must continually cry out to God
with your whole heart, *"Not my will, but Thy will be done."*
This is the crossroads where the Church stands today.**

THE TIME FOR 'MIGHTY MEN'

I believe that since we live in the last days, we will begin to see more and more of God's power manifested in this earth. Nothing will be able to stop this great outpouring of the Holy Spirit. The gates of hell cannot prevail against what is happening in our midst.

No man, no organization, no government, and no natural disaster can stop this move that God has begun.

God is raising up "mighty men" in this hour — those men and women who know what it is to fight on the devil's territory. They know what it is to get behind the lines of battle. They are the ones coming on the scene to shake the Church and demand action from those in the pews.

I say, "Let the Church shake!"

The prophets of Almighty God are coming out of obscurity. They are emerging with messages that will stir the hearts of men and women as never before. Their messages will cause governments to shake. Their words will bring godly fear upon those who hear them.

These fiery men and women of God will speak with great boldness. They will not simply present messages with steps one, two, and three. They will speak boldly about living a godly lifestyle. They will speak on developing a strong prayer life. They will speak out against sin. They will speak out against the things of the world that have crept into our churches, such as gossip, hate, idolatry, and sexual immorality.

I believe God is going to speak to His Church as never before. Those who will shake the earth for Him will be those who are dead to self. They will know how to ascend to the throne of God and get plans for the battle. They will not wait for the enemy to attack, because they will already be invading enemy territory according to the strategic plans and timings of Heaven.

It is time for the Church to take the kingdom of darkness by force. It is time for people in the pews to stand up and let their voices sound out among the nations! It is time for both young and old to join hands with God and let the glory of God manifest throughout the whole earth. It is time for the earth to know that He demands holiness and righteousness

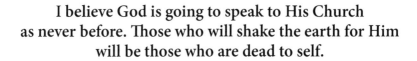

I believe God is going to speak to His Church
as never before. Those who will shake the earth for Him
will be those who are dead to self.

Our Greatest Weapon —
The Law of Love

God has spiritual laws that we must observe in our daily lives, and none is greater than the law of love. Jesus talked to His disciples about this divine commandment in John 13:34:

A new commandment I give unto you, that ye love one another; as I have loved you, that ye also love one another.

If you walk in love, you will not sin. If you walk in love, you will live right; you will talk right; you will be right. However, if you say you are walking in love, but then you sin on Saturday night and show up in church looking "holy" on Sunday morning, God does not agree with you.

You cannot get in the pulpit and preach a Holy Spirit sermon when you have sinned on Saturday night with pornography. You cannot preach a Holy Spirit sermon unless things are right in your life.

God loves His people enough to discipline them, and the Church must be willing to receive His correction. Many churches have gone without correction for far too long.

165

Anytime a child goes without correction, that child will get into more trouble. In the same way, many congregations are in chaos because ministers have not spoken the truth as God spoke it to them. Too many who stand in the pulpit have held back from proclaiming the truth because of the fear of man. They are afraid to offend those who are influential through finances or popularity.

We must be like Jeremiah and Ezekiel. When the Lord says, "Speak," we must speak!

**Too many who stand in the pulpit
have held back from proclaiming the truth
because of the fear of man.**

God no longer asks people to die to self; He commands it. He no longer asks people to live in holiness; He commands it. Actually, He has commanded it all along, but we have no time to play games anymore with what God requires because the Church Age is coming to a close.

When time stops, wherever you are found is where you will be judged. If you have died to self, you will be in that special spot that God has ordained for you. Nothing can stop you if you live and abide in the presence of the Almighty!

Part 4

HOLDING FAST
TO THE WORD
OF THE LORD

CHAPTER 13

When Logic and Faith Collide

O nce you die to self, you must hold fast to the word of the Lord and obey whatever God tells you to do *when* He tells you to do it.

Picture this: You're sitting in a boat, far out on a lake and miles away from the nearest shore. Suddenly you hear the unmistakable voice of God: *"Get out of the boat and walk on the water."*

What would you do?

First, you might slap yourself up the side of your head to make sure you weren't hearing things! But suppose even after you did that, the voice came again, sounding just as persistent and loud as before.

"Get out of the boat and walk on the water."

There would be only one thing to do in a situation like that: You'd have to immediately get out of the boat and start walking on the water, just as the voice of God had instructed you to do.

That's what happened to Peter. When he stepped out of the boat, he was making a very illogical and silly-looking move in the eyes of anyone who may have been watching. But as long as Peter responded in faith, the water might as well have been solid ground, because it supported his body without a bit of trouble.

However, as soon as Peter took his eyes off Jesus and looked at what he was doing from a logical perspective, he got in big trouble. Peter began to sink as if he were wearing concrete boots!

I don't think it's likely that God is going to tell you to go walking across the nearest lake — but then again, He might! Whatever God has called you to do, you can expect to experience moments when His direct word or instruction to you will collide with the world's notion of logic and good sense.

Other people may tell you that you'd be foolish to follow the Lord's instruction because it doesn't make sense to their natural reasoning. Your own mind may tell you that you'd be foolish to obey. But it's never foolish to keep holding fast to God's specific word to you. Never in a billion years can you make a wrong move by doing what He tells you to do.

The truth is, when natural logic collides with a direct word from God, logic crumbles into a pile of tiny pieces while the word He spoke to you remains solid, unbroken, and unmoved.

Biblical Examples of Those Who Defied Logic To Obey God

The Bible is full of examples of people who were willing to follow God's specific word to them, even when it defied natural logic, and were then blessed beyond measure because of their obedience.

**When natural logic collides
with a direct word from God,
logic crumbles into a pile of tiny pieces
while the word He spoke to you
remains solid, unbroken, and unmoved.**

For example, it wasn't logical for a humble shepherd named Moses to go before the mighty Pharaoh and demand that the children of Israel be set free. But that's what God told Moses to do, so that's what Moses did. And because of Moses' obedience to the Lord, the Israelites were able to leave Egypt and make their way to the Promised Land (*see* Exod. chapters 3-12).

It wasn't logical for Noah to build a huge boat far from the nearest ocean. But he was obeying God's specific command to him when he did it, and as a result, only Noah and his family survived a worldwide calamity (*see* Gen. chapters 6-9).

It wasn't logical for Gideon to go up against the fury of the entire Midianite army with a tiny group of men armed only with pitchers and trumpets. But Gideon did what the word of the Lord commanded, and as a result, the nation of Israel threw off its oppressors and gained its independence (*see* Judges 6:12-7:25).

Abraham is a great example of someone who believed God's Word in spite of what his natural mind told him. Romans 4:3 (NKJV) tells us that "...Abraham believed God, and it was accounted to him for righteousness."

Therefore it is of faith that it might be according to grace, so that the promise might be sure to all the seed, not only to those who are of the law, but also to those who are of the faith of Abraham, who is the father of us all (as it is written, "I have made you a father of many nations") in the presence of Him whom he believed — God, who gives life to the dead and calls those things which do not exist as though they did; who, contrary to hope, in hope believed, so that he became the father of many nations, according to what was spoken, "So shall your descendants be."

And not being weak in faith, he did not consider his own body, already dead (since he was about a hundred years old), and the deadness of Sarah's womb. He did not waver at the promise of God through unbelief, but was strengthened in faith, giving glory to God, and being fully convinced that what He had promised He was also able to perform.

Romans 4:16-21 NKJV

It wasn't logical for Abraham to believe God's promise that he would be the father of many nations. After all, Abraham didn't have any children, and he and his wife Sarah were well past the age of childbearing. Abraham could have looked at himself, shaken his head, and said, "Lord, You must have me mixed up with someone else."

But Abraham didn't do that, and he did indeed become the father of many nations, just as God had promised he would (*see* Gen. 17:4). It was through the lineage of Abraham that Jesus Christ came into the world in the flesh so all of us who have surrendered our lives to Christ can consider ourselves to be sons and daughters of Abraham (*see* Matt. 1:17; Gal. 3:7).

Hold Fast
to What God Has Told You

God may be speaking to you about doing something for Him that seems impossible, just as He spoke to Moses, Noah, and Abraham. Like these men of God, you may be struggling to trust God's word to you in the midst of the very real circumstances that surround you.

I have experienced those same kinds of struggles in my own walk with God.

For example, when I was still a young boy, the Lord told me that He was going to send me to the nations to preach for Him. My logical mind said, *What's this about going around the world for God? You don't even own a car! And even if you did, you couldn't afford enough gas to get to the other side of town, much less travel to the other side of the world!*

In spite of the doubts that assailed me, I clung fast to the word that the Lord had spoken to me. I bought a map of the world and hung it on my wall. Then every morning when I got up to get ready for school, I would hit that map and say, "I'm coming to you — open up!"

I kept doing that day after day, even though some days my head would tell me that I was crazy. And do you know what? Over the years, God has taken me to 127 countries — and I'm still counting! I have traveled throughout the world on assignment to proclaim salvation through Jesus Christ and to train up a new generation of leaders to bring revival and reformation to the Church.

At first, it wasn't easy for me to get used to traveling so much. If I'd had my own way, I'd rather have stayed home where I was comfortable.

Traveling can be very hard on the human body, especially when you're always going back and forth across time zones and experiencing jet lag. Sometimes you can't remember what day it is, much less what time it is. It seems like you're always standing in lines, looking for your luggage, and trying to get used to the local food and customs.

I was always so glad when I returned home to the United States where I could drink the water right out of the tap without worrying about getting sick and flip a switch to enjoy electric lighting any time of the day or night. But although the traveling was often exhausting, I loved having the opportunity to meet people in other countries and tell them about Jesus.

After a while, the inconveniences of traveling didn't seem so bad as I began to see the harvest come in from the seeds I had planted. Besides, the desire to preach the Gospel was so strong in me that I'd begin to feel antsy and unfulfilled if I wasn't out on the road. I wanted to be busy doing what God had called me to do according to His plan and His timings.

TRUST GOD TO MAKE THE 'IMPOSSIBLE' A REALITY

Then later the Lord spoke to me again: *"Roberts, I want you to build a school for My glory."*

But, Lord, my mind protested, *I'm spending so much time on the road. How in the world could I ever build a school for You?*

Nevertheless, the Lord's voice was persistent, and I knew I had to obey. So as He had commanded, I founded a Bible school where young men and women would be taught how to be effective ministers of the Gospel. It meant an entirely new direction for me. It also meant that I couldn't travel as much, which felt strange at first. But then came the peaceful assurance that always accompanies obedience.

Has God spoken a specific thing for you to do? Perhaps He has given you an assignment that isn't even in the same ballpark of what you're doing right now. You may be thinking, *Well, I sure don't see how that's going to happen.*

But you don't have to see how God's plan is going to come to pass in your life. You just have to trust Him. You have to stay assured that His Word is always true and what He has proclaimed for you *will* come to pass if you stay obedient and yielded to the leading of His Spirit.

Another thing to keep in mind is that you cannot dictate to God how and when things are going to work out. You can't tell Him, "Lord, this is the way I want You to do it." You simply must stay yielded and obedient to Him.

God is not a cosmic errand boy who jumps when we call His name. He is a loving Father who wants only the best for us as He molds us into what He created us to be. It's truly amazing what God can do in our lives when we actually believe His Word.

In the early years of my ministry, I hosted a big convention in Minneapolis, Minnesota. When I first began this venture, I was worried because we had so many big-name speakers coming in and our expenses were going to run more than $100,000 for the week. That was a lot of money for me.

You cannot dictate to God how and when things are going to work out. You can't tell Him, "Lord, this is the way I want You to do it." You simply must stay yielded and obedient to Him.

I kept thinking, *What if no one comes? What are we going to do if we can't pay our bill? What if I'm being presumptuous or foolish?*

But that was just fear trying to torment my mind, because I knew in my spirit that I was doing exactly what God had told me to do. Deep down inside, I knew there wouldn't be any problem in paying the bills and blessing the ministries of the speakers who had been asked to participate in the convention. Nevertheless, I really had to wield the sword of the Word to stay steady, because my soul and my flesh were fighting against my faith. And by the end of the convention, God had shown Himself faithful, with all expenses paid in full!

Every time I go somewhere to preach a series of messages, conduct a seminar, or speak at a convention, my natural mind always asks, *What if no one comes?* But then the meetings start, and the people come. I always look around and think, *Wow! Just look at all these people! They really came!*

I often have to remind myself that when I am doing what God has asked me to do *His* way and in *His* timing, He is always faithful to honor my obedience.

What God Said, He Will Do!

We serve the most awesome, powerful God. He spoke this entire universe into existence! We just can't go wrong when we're following Him.

Several years ago, I read a true story written by the mother of a little boy who was in the third grade. This mom was listening to her son say his prayers one night and was shocked to hear him say, "And, thank You, Lord, that You're going to let me fly."

When the mother questioned her young son about his prayer, he said he was certain that God had spoken to him that he was going to be able to fly.

"You mean on a big airplane, like when we go to see your grandpa?" his mother asked him.

"No, like this," the little boy replied, and he began flapping his arms like a bird.

Naturally, the mother didn't know what to do. After all, she knew little boys can't fly by flapping their arms. But she had worked so hard to build up her son's faith; she didn't want to do or say anything that might damage it.

In the weeks that followed, the young boy kept believing that he was going to be able to flap his wings and fly around the room. His faith never wavered. Then one day, he came home from school all excited. It seemed his class was going to put on a performance of Peter Pan, and he had been selected for the starring role!

When the day of the performance came, the mother and her son saw God's word fulfilled. The school had rigged up a contraption consisting of ropes and pulleys whereby Peter Pan was able to "fly" around the room. The little boy was absolutely beside himself with delight. As soon as the performance was over, he ran into his mother's arms and said, "See? I told you that God said He was going to let me fly!"

Now, you may be thinking that it's a very long way from the fulfillment of God's word for that little boy to the fulfillment of what God has spoken to you. But is it really?

And he [Jesus] **said: "Truly I tell you, unless you change and become like little children, you will never enter the kingdom of heaven."**

Matthew 18:3 NIV

Perhaps God has been calling you to do something great for His Kingdom, but as you look at yourself, you want to say, "How, Lord? I can't do something like that." Oh, yes, you can. If you will accept and believe God's word to you with the simple, unquestioning faith of a child, you will see His glory manifested in your life!

The Voice Worth Listening To

Think back to Abraham. What did he do when God spoke to him? Abraham began to speak the same language God was speaking. Abraham agreed with God that what He had said was true: "Yes, Lord, I believe I will be the father of many nations."

When God speaks to you, your language must begin to echo His language.

When Abraham first began to say, "I am the father of many nations," I'm sure his friends and neighbors must have thought he was totally out of his mind. Can't you picture them pointing at him and laughing behind his back? "Poor old guy has really lost his mind. He doesn't even have one child, and he thinks he's the father of many nations."

When God speaks to you, your language must begin to echo His language.

But Abraham just let people say what they were going to say about him and kept holding fast to his faith. He didn't know how or when the word of the Lord was going to be fulfilled, but he knew it was going to happen.

Plenty of people in this world like nothing better than to run around trampling on other people's dreams. They don't want God's word to others to come true or for others to succeed, because then they will feel left behind. But don't listen to the naysayers — listen to God!

It's easy to hold on to a word from the Lord when everyone around you agrees with it. It's not so easy when they are vehement in their opposition to it.

When I was still in my teens, God called me into the ministry. He wasn't telling me that He wanted me to go into the ministry *someday*. He was telling me that He wanted me to start preaching *immediately*.

Not everyone was thrilled with the idea of a boy preacher. I heard comments like, "You're too young to be a preacher," and, "Are you sure you're really listening to God?" Some people thought I was being presumptuous or was getting carried away with a sense of my own importance. They wanted me to "know my place" and stay there, doing the things that "normal" teenagers do.

It's easy to hold on to a word from the Lord when everyone around you agrees with it. It's not so easy when they are vehement in their opposition to it.

But it didn't matter to me what anyone else said. Even at that early age, I knew that God's voice was the only voice really worth listening to. I began preaching in churches throughout my hometown of Tulsa, Oklahoma, and as a result of my obedience to God's word to me, I saw hundreds of people come to salvation through faith in Jesus Christ.

BEWARE THE CRITICS

Unfortunately, this world of ours is full of critics. My definition of a critic is someone who can't or won't try to do anything himself but gets great delight in passing judgment on others who do try to accomplish things.

Critics say things like, "This guy isn't much of a teacher," but they won't volunteer to teach. Or they might say, "Can you believe she had the nerve to sing a solo in church with her voice?" — but they're not about to get up and use their own voice to glorify God. Critics say, "This fellow has a lot of nerve, thinking that God told him to start a Bible school," but they don't take the time to listen to what God might be saying to *them*.

Some people see the negative in every situation. We give them some good news, and they quickly respond with their favorite saying: "Yes, but..."

- "Yes, but what about this?"

- "Yes, but have you thought about that?"

- "Yes, but what if such-and-such happens?"

Sometimes I've just had to look someone like that right in the eye and say, "Please just be quiet in Jesus' Name!"

I would get so happy and excited when God spoke to me about a future part of His plan for me that I'd scarcely be able to contain my joy. But then some of my friends would start raising their objections: "But, Roberts, what about this or that?" Their arguments were terribly disappointing because I hadn't asked for a dissecting of the word I had received from the Lord. I wanted my friends to be excited with me regarding what God was going to do in my life!

Abraham didn't ask God to give him pages of explanation on how it was going to be possible for him and Sarah to have a child at their advanced age. He just believed and agreed with God that he would be the father of many nations.

Abraham didn't look at Sarah and say, "No way!" Sarah didn't look at him and say, "That's right. No way!" Abraham and Sarah held fast to what God had said to them.

> He [Abraham] **staggered not at the promise of God through unbelief; but was strong in faith, giving glory to God; and being fully persuaded that, what he had promised, he was able also to perform.**
>
> **Romans 4:20-21**

What does it mean to be *fully persuaded*? I like the way Oral Roberts defined it: "It means that you know that you know that you know that you know that you *know* it's so." That's the way it was for Abraham.

As you pursue God's will, you may find yourself surrounded by critics and naysayers. But you have to keep in mind that if God has told you to do something, He knows that you have the ability and the resources to do it. You can be assured that He will work through you to accomplish His purpose in your life. All that God has planned for you will come to pass in His timing as you stay yielded to Him.

Are people criticizing you and saying negative things about you because you are holding fast to God's Word? Read on to find out what critics have said about some other familiar people.

- Early in Lucille Ball's career, a movie producer told her that she had absolutely no acting talent and she ought to forget about being in show business. Lucille didn't listen, and all of us who have laughed at her antics over the years are very glad she didn't.

- A publishing company sent a letter to a novice author by the name of Zane Grey, telling him that he couldn't write and would never be able to write, and that they wished he would stop wasting their time with his material. But Grey kept on writing and wound up with literally dozens of bestsellers, selling millions of books.

- Thomas Edison's father believed his son to be a "dunce" and once whipped the boy in public for his failures at school.

- When Ludwig van Beethoven was a boy, his piano teacher pronounced him as being "hopeless" and said he had no musical ability whatsoever.

I could go on with page after page of other examples — people who refused to listen to their critics and instead continued to pursue their dreams. I am not saying that all the people I have listed were particularly godly or that they were following what God had told them to do. I don't know about that one way or the other. But I do know that they all found success using their God-given talents after making the choice not to listen to their critics.

You'll do the same — especially with God on your side! Listen to God's word to you rather than the words of the critics and the naysayers. As you do, your faith will be built up until you're able to see past the barriers and the obstacles that might otherwise keep you from finishing the work God has called you to fulfill. Romans 10:17 says, "Faith cometh by hearing, and hearing by the word of God."

**All that God has planned for you
will come to pass in His timing
as you stay yielded to Him.**

Faith causes things to happen, and Abraham was not weak in faith. He built up his faith by holding fast to God's promise and rehearsing to himself what God had said to him.

Abraham could have focused on the negatives: "I'm an old man. Sarah is an old woman. We've been married all these years without having any children, so how in the world can I believe I'm going to have a son now?" Instead, he stayed focused on God's Word to him: *"You will be the father of many nations."*

I am surprised at how many people in the modern world try to tell God what to think and how to act. Our society is full of people trying to act like Jehovah. When you begin to obey, that's when they start to criticize: "Well, I just don't think you ought to do that."

Those people need to think less and to believe and obey more. The Bible says that Abraham *held* to faith. He built himself up, not being weak in faith. "…He considered not his own body now dead…" (Rom. 4:19). Abraham lived in faith that what God had said to him would come to pass, no matter how long it took or how impossible it may have looked to those who were seeing only through physical eyes.

**Faith causes things to happen, and Abraham
was not weak in faith. He built up his faith by holding fast
to God's promise and rehearsing to himself
what God had said to him.**

Always remember that your security is in the Word of God. There is no security in how much money you have, what kind of car you drive, or how fancy your home is. There is no security in your career or the investments you make. There isn't even any security in the relationships you have with other people.

Your money may be stolen; your house may burn down; you may lose your job; and your investments may go sour. Even your friends and loved ones may disappoint you. Security is found in only one place in this world, and that is in the abiding Word of God.

I don't mean to imply that God's Word won't be challenging. It may shake you out of your routine or rock your comfort zone. Nevertheless, you can know beyond a shadow of a doubt that following and obeying the Word of God is the only possible source of lasting security.

Some in the Charismatic Movement have gotten to the point where they believe that God speaks to them only with nice, sweet, encouraging words. In their thinking, He only says things like, *"Oh, My people, I love you. Hang in there, and everything will be all right. I know life can be hard sometimes. But remember that I love you, and it will help you get through."*

I'm not doubting God's love for a moment, and I do believe that He wants us all to be encouraged and strengthened by His presence in our lives. But I know that God is also calling us to boldness and action on His behalf.

You can know beyond a shadow of a doubt that following and obeying the Word of God is the only possible source of lasting security.

He may tell you something like, *"I want you to build a big church for Me."*

"Who, me?" you respond with surprise.

"Yes, you."

"Oh, uh… well, I thought God was talking to me, but it must have been the devil. After all, God only says things like, *'Be encouraged. Be at peace. I love you.'*"

The God we serve is not like that. He often says things like:

- *"I want you to go into other nations and preach the Gospel."*

- *"I want you to feed the poor in My Name."*

- *"I want you to get involved in a crisis pregnancy center and help save lives."*

- *"I want you to become a missionary."*

But some of us answer, "What? Me? Listen, Lord, You must not know me very well. I can't start a church for You! Why, I can hardly pay my light bill! My children are in rebellion. My life is so mixed up and confused. Please don't ask me to do something great for You!"

Let me tell you, if God didn't see in you the ability and capacity to do great things for Him, He wouldn't ask you to do those things. God knows the greatness He has built into you, and He wants to work in you and through you to develop and utilize your supply.

What is God saying to you? Whatever His word is to you, make the decision to believe it and act upon it, and just watch what happens!

God knows the greatness He has built into you, and He wants to work in you and through you to develop and utilize your supply.

CHAPTER 11

Don't Ever Let Go,
Even in a Victory

When the Apostle Peter began walking on the water, he soon became distracted by the wind and the waves. When he shifted his focus, Peter momentarily lost his faith and began to sink like a rock.

Undoubtedly that moment was forever etched in Peter's mind as one of his biggest failures — yet it actually started out as one of his greatest successes. Peter was doing what no other man has ever done, with the exception of Jesus. Peter was walking on top of the Sea of Galilee like someone out for a Sunday afternoon stroll! Imagine how the apostles felt when they saw Peter get out of that boat and start walking on the water.

"Look at Peter — he's actually walking on the water! Can you believe it?"

I'm sure the apostles were thrilled and amazed by their friend's courage, but that's not where the story ended. In Peter's moment of victory, he let go of God's word, and his ultimate failure swallowed up his initial triumph.

Don't Let Go of What God Has Said!

I have seen that sort of thing happen so many times. Sometimes people let go of God's word because the success that has come their way surprises them. They think, like Peter did, *I can't really be doing this! Something's bound to go wrong. I just know it's all going to fall apart.* And when their fears become stronger than their faith, it does fall apart.

In Peter's moment of victory, he let go of God's word, and his ultimate failure swallowed up his initial triumph.

Other people have let go of God's word because they've become overly confident. They've built up some kind of personal empire that seems to be running well, and they get to the point where they no longer think they need to listen to God. The Lord may even be telling them that it's time to move on in an entirely new direction, but they're not listening. Instead, they're doing the same old thing, only now they're trying to do it in their own power instead of in God's power, and that always spells disaster.

Some people tend to look at God in the same way a child would look at a parent who is teaching him how to ride a bicycle. Dad's running along behind his little boy, who is trying his best to keep the handlebars steady and pedal at the same time. Finally, Dad gives a big push and the youngster is riding on his own. "Thanks, Dad, but I don't need your help anymore!" the boy yells as he pedals down the street.

That's something we can *never* say to God: "Thanks, but I don't need Your help anymore." We always need His help! As long as you and I are living on this planet, we are going to face challenges and hurdles. Satan will never stop trying to bump us off the path of God's plan or pull us out of His timing. That means there's *never* a time when it's okay to let go of His instruction or His hand of guidance to get you where He needs you to go.

Even When God's Request Doesn't Seem To Make Sense

Sometimes the Lord may tell you to do something that seems totally contradictory to everything else He has asked you to do. If this is the case, there are a couple of points to keep in mind.

The first is that the Lord is the only One who knows how things are going to come together in your life. He is the only One who sees the twists and turns that will be necessary to get you to where He wants you to be.

The second point is that God may be working on purifying your motives. In other words, He wants to ensure that you are holding to His word because you believe and trust Him no matter what, *not* because you are only looking for the things He can give you.

The Lord is the only One who knows how things are going to come together in your life. He is the only One who sees the twists and turns that will be necessary to get you to where He wants you to be.

To explain what I'm talking about, let's take a look at Abraham and Isaac. We've already talked about how Abraham believed God's promise that he would become the father of many nations, even though he and his wife were both old and had no children.

And true to the word of the Lord, Sarah eventually conceived and gave birth to Isaac.

I hope that when Isaac was born, Abraham and Sarah threw a huge party to celebrate. I hope they invited all of the people who had said earlier, "Abraham, you're crazy to go around saying God told you that you would be the father of many nations! You must be delirious. God hasn't spoken to you."

I'm sure it would have given Abraham a great deal of satisfaction to show off his baby boy and say things like, "Would you like to hold my delusion for a while? Hey, you who ridiculed me the most, how would you like to change his diapers?" How good it must have been for Abraham to be able to say, "See what God can do! He is always true to His word!"

But then consider what happened several years later. God said, 'Abraham, I want you to go out into the wilderness to offer Me a sacrifice — your son, Isaac" (*see* Gen. 22:2).

Imagine how Abraham must have felt when he heard those words. He had waited so long for this little boy to be born. He had held on to God's promise that he would become the father of many nations, even when his friends and neighbors laughed at him. And as a very old man, he had been experiencing for the very first time the joy of a developing father-son relationship. He was discovering what a wonderful, irreplaceable feeling parental love can be.

Then God said to Abraham, "I want you to show Me how much you love Me by giving Me the life of your only son."

What would you have done if you were Abraham? Most of us would have probably thrown what my mother used to call a "conniption fit."

"*What are You talking about, Lord?* How can You ask me to do something like this? All of my friends thought I was a nut for believing You when You said that I was going to be a father, and now they're really going to think I'm a bigger nut if I offer my only son as a sacrifice. I just can't do it! I *won't* do it!"

You see, Abraham had attained his goal. He had become a father. But then came the next challenge — a test to see whether he was willing to sacrifice everything in order to obey God.

> **By faith Abraham, when he was tested, offered up Isaac, and he who had received the promises offered up his only begotten son, of whom it was said, "In Isaac your seed shall be called," concluding that God was able to raise him**

up, even from the dead, from which he also received him in a figurative sense.

Hebrews 11:17-19 NKJV

Imagine Abraham walking out of his home that morning on his way to offer a sacrifice to the Lord. His servants are with him; Isaac is with him. But there isn't any animal being led along to provide a sacrifice — no ram, goat, or bull. Picture young Isaac running on ahead of everyone, doing the things that boys do — throwing rocks, kicking at sticks and leaves, and asking a hundred questions, such as, "Dad, what are we going to sacrifice?"

Abraham answers softly, "It's okay, Son. We'll find something to sacrifice. God will provide." Yet Abraham knows all the while that his precious son is going to be placed upon that altar.

Nevertheless, Abraham will not allow himself to be dissuaded from holding fast to the word of the Lord or from his faith that God always knows what is right and best. God said, "I want you to give Me your son," and Abraham is prepared to give God his son. It's that simple.

So this little procession arrives at the spot where the sacrifice is to take place. Abraham piles the wood on top of the altar and makes other preparations for the sacrifice, and little Isaac is looking around, more perplexed than ever. "I don't understand, Dad. We don't have any animals with us."

And Abraham is forced to say, "My son, you are the sacrifice." Having said that, Abraham ties up the boy, places him on the altar, and prepares to strike him dead with his knife. But it is precisely at that moment, and not a moment sooner, that an angel stops Abraham. The angel tells him that God doesn't want him to offer the boy as a sacrifice; He was only testing Abraham's faithfulness.

Abraham didn't know that was going to happen. When he raised his knife to strike his son, he didn't understand why this was what God commanded, but he was willing to do it anyway. And he was still believing God's promise that he would be the father of many nations. Hebrews 11:19 tells us what Abraham was thinking — that God would raise Isaac from the dead if necessary to fulfill His promise.

In the natural, there was no way for Abraham to fit all the pieces together. They just did not make sense. But Abraham was willing to say, "Lord, I don't understand it, but You do. And I can't do anything other than trust You."

You see, similar things will happen in your life as you face challenges and different forms of opposition. It will look as if everything will be destroyed instead of built up if you do what God is telling you to do. Persecutions and accusations will come along, designed to weaken you in the faith and make you withdraw from the word that the Lord has given you. You will be hit in your spirit with a great temptation to loosen your grasp on God's word to you and to start holding on to natural things. But if you let go of that word, you will gradually shrivel up and die from the inside out!

I have held on to what God has said to me and have not let go of it. I've been hit, and I've had victories. I have learned that whatever seems to be happening, whether it is good or bad, the most important thing I can do is to hold on to God's Word. It is my foundation and my security!

I have learned that whatever seems to be happening, whether it is good or bad, the most important thing I can do is to hold on to God's Word. It is my foundation and my security!

"Roberts, do you know what you're doing?"

"Yes, I'm doing what God has told me to do."

"But do you understand what the outcome of this will be?"

"No, I don't need to understand that. All I need to know is that God told me to do it, and He expects me to obey."

Don't Question — Just Obey!

Obedience to God is the key. It's not important for us to understand *why* God wants us to do something. We just have to know *what* He is telling us to do and *when* He is telling us to do it — and then to be willing to obey.

As we can see from the life of Abraham, it is not always easy to hold fast to the word of the Lord. In fact, it can be terribly, terribly difficult. In fact, the Bible has many accounts of people who tried to run away from God's word to them, but who ultimately found their destinies as a result of their obedience.

- Moses didn't want to obey when God told him that he had been chosen to bring the children of Israel out of Egypt. Moses said something like this: "But, Lord, you know how tongue-tied I can get. When I'm standing before Pharaoh, I'll start stammering and stuttering, and I'll make a complete fool of myself. I really don't think that will convince him that I'm a representative of the One who created the universe!" (*see* Exod. 4:10).

But, eventually, Moses agreed to do things God's way, and he became the great leader of an entire nation.

- When the word of God came to a young man named Saul, telling him that he had been chosen to be the first king of Israel, Saul tried to hide among some baggage (*see* 1 Sam. 10:21-22). Saul must have been thinking something like, *What? Me, a king? God, You must have me mixed up with someone else. I don't want the job. Please find someone else — I'm not qualified!*

  But God would not be dissuaded from His choice of Saul, and Saul went on to lead Israel in a number of great military victories (*see* 1 Sam. 14:47-48).

- God told Gideon he had been chosen to lead the Israelites into battle against their oppressors, the Midianites. Gideon's reply was that he couldn't do it because he came from the least of the families of Israel and was the least one in that least family.

  But God knew the man He was choosing, and Gideon went on to prove on the battlefield that His choice was the correct one (*see* Judges 6-8).

There are other examples in the Word of individuals who didn't agree with God that they were the right choice for the task required.

- Jonah tried to run in the opposite direction when God told him to go preach repentance to the people who lived in Nineveh (*see* Jonah 1:1-3).

- Jeremiah told God he couldn't speak to the people because he was only a youth (*see* Jer. 1:6).

- Elijah fled into the wilderness and hid because he thought he was the only one left who was on God's side (*see* 1 Kings 19:14).

**It's not important for us to understand
why God wants us to do something.
We just have to know *what* He is telling us to do
and *when* He is telling us to do it —
and then to be willing to obey.**

NEVER STOP LISTENING AND OBEYING

Take a closer look at the lives of some of these heroes from the Bible, and you'll find out that they stumbled not at the beginning of their walk with the Lord, but much later on when they had gained a bit more confidence and were flush with the heady feeling of success.

For example, it wasn't until Moses struck a rock to get water for the people, instead of speaking to the rock as God had commanded him, that he got into trouble. It seemed natural to Moses to strike the rock because he had done it so many times before.

But this time God had clearly told Moses to speak to the rock and the water would pour forth. Moses wasn't listening — or possibly he acted out of his own anger and frustration with the people's complaints. Regardless, he did the wrong thing, and as a result, he was not allowed to enter the Promised Land (*see* Num. 20:8-12).

The same thing happened with King Saul. God ordered him to destroy all of the Amalekites, but Saul didn't listen. As a result, the kingdom was taken away from Saul and given to David (*see* 1 Sam. 15:1-29).

Then there was Gideon. Fresh from his victory on the battlefield, Gideon fashioned an idol, which then became a snare to Gideon and to his house (*see* Judges 8:22-28).

Note that it wasn't in the beginning that these individuals stumbled; it was when they were gaining confidence. They were feeling pretty good about themselves. Perhaps they thought they didn't need to listen all that closely to the word of the Lord anymore.

I don't know of anyone who doesn't need to listen to the word of the Lord. There are a lot of people who aren't listening to what God has to say, and that's why the world is in such a mess.

Remember the old commercial that said, "When E. F. Hutton speaks, everyone listens"? Wouldn't this world of ours be a wonderful place if it were true that when God spoke, everyone listened? It's not going to happen this side of the Millennial Reign, but it can happen on a personal level in your life. There is peace, prosperity, and joy in following the word of the Lord.

...Man does not live on bread alone but on every word that comes from the mouth of the Lord.

Deuteronomy 8:3 NIV

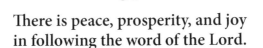

**There is peace, prosperity, and joy
in following the word of the Lord.**

Make a decision that from this day on, you will hold tightly to God's word for you. This is a decision you will never regret!

CHAPTER

Why You Don't Need
a 'Plan B'

et's take another look at Peter sitting in the boat on the
Sea of Galilee. He looked up and saw Jesus walking
toward him, coming right over the top of the water.

"Lord," he cried, "if it's You, let me get out of the boat and walk to You."

And Jesus simply replied, "Come."

Peter immediately climbed out of the boat and started walking on the water, heading toward Jesus.

Admittedly, Peter didn't get very far. The Bible tells us that this event took place on a very windy night and that the wind and the waves took Peter's attention away from his Lord and caused him to begin to sink. But what ended up as a rather spectacular failure started out as a brilliant triumph of faith. For a while, Peter was dancing over those waves like there was nothing to it.

I admire Peter for having the faith and the courage to get out of the boat in the first place. I also admire him for the speed with which he followed his Lord's command to "come."

What ended up as a rather spectacular failure started out as a brilliant triumph of faith. For a while, Peter was dancing over those waves like there was nothing to it.

Peter didn't spend a moment trying to put together an alternative plan. He didn't say, "Okay, Lord, I'll be right there — but just in case it doesn't work, let me look around here and see if I can find a flotation device." He didn't even turn to the other disciples and say, "Okay, guys, I'm going to get out of this boat and try to walk on the water. But if it doesn't work, I want you all to be ready to haul me back in." No, Peter just got out of that boat and started walking across the water!

I believe that far too many people today miss God's timing because they're only halfhearted in their obedience to His word to them. They say, "Okay, Lord, I hear You and I'm willing to follow. But just the same, I think I better have a couple of alternatives in mind in the event that what You have planned for me doesn't work out."

Such thinking shows a complete lack of understanding of the power and faithfulness of God. To spend time and effort trying to figure out a "Plan B" in case God's plan doesn't work out can only lead to trouble.

'Plan B' Always Leads to Trouble

Consider what happened between Abraham and Sarah before they settled in and stood fast in faith for the manifestation of God's promise. Sarah thought that a "Plan B" was necessary to fulfill God's promise to her husband. The Bible doesn't give us a word-for-word description of her conversation with Abraham, but I imagine it went something like this: "Look, Abraham, we both know that God has promised to make you the father of many nations. We also know that I'm well past the age when I can have a baby. But Hagar, my handmaiden — now, there's a woman who is still in the prime of life. She could be the one to have your baby. I really think you should think seriously about that" (*see* Gen. 16:1).

Abraham, like millions of other husbands before and since his day, was willing to do just about anything his wife wanted him to do. So he slept with Hagar, and she became pregnant and gave birth to a son whom she named Ishmael (*see* Gen. 16:4-16).

But God's promise was to Abraham and to *Sarah*, and He didn't need them to help Him out in fulfilling that promise. When they did put a "Plan B" of their own making into place, the whole thing backfired terribly. The situation led to strife between Sarah and Hagar, and then between the descendants of Ishmael and Isaac (*see* Gen. 25:18).

That strife has continued through the centuries and right up to the present day, for the Jewish race descended from Isaac, and through Ishmael, the Arab nation was born. Certainly it was Sarah and Abraham's rashness in believing they had to help God out by devising a "Plan B" that led to centuries of trouble.

> **God's promise was to Abraham and to Sarah, and He didn't need them to help Him out in fulfilling that promise. When they did put a "Plan B" of their own making into place, the whole thing backfired terribly.**

You may remember another time in the Bible when someone thought there was a need for a "Plan B" and it resulted in a whole bunch of trouble. That someone was Aaron, the brother of Moses.

Moses had gone up on the mountain to receive instruction from the Lord that included the Ten Commandments. In his absence, the people of Israel grew impatient. They didn't know when and if Moses was coming back, and they were tired of following after an "invisible" God. They wanted something they could see and touch.

In the end, Aaron bowed under the pressure of the people's discontent and looked for a way to pacify them. Gathering up all the gold from everyone's possessions, Aaron had the gold melted down and fashioned into the shape of a calf; then he presented it to them as the god who had brought them out of Egypt (*see* Exod. 32:1).

Such blasphemy! The children of Israel had seen the plagues God had brought upon the nation of Egypt. They had seen

Him part the Red Sea so they could pass through it. They had watched the waves come crashing down on the heads of the Egyptians who tried to pursue them. They had seen the pillar of fire by night and the cloud of smoke by day, leading them to the Promised Land.

Yet with all that the children of Israel had witnessed of God's power to save them, they were ready to trade the glory of the living God for a statue of a cow. Talk about trading a glorious "Plan A" for a pathetic "Plan B"! And, of course, the results were disastrous.

With all that the children of Israel had witnessed of God's power to save them, they were ready to trade the glory of the living God for a statue of a cow.

God's 'Plan A' — It's Only a Matter of Time

In the world of faith, there is simply no need to have "Plan B" in your back pocket, because God's "Plan A" *always* works. The most important thing is to spend time praying and meditating on the Word so you have a clear understanding of "Plan A."

I admit that it isn't always easy to follow God's plan for your life. There will be times when, from a natural perspective, it may seem downright scary. But you have to keep your eyes focused on Jesus instead of on the wind and the waves. No matter what your circumstances appear to be, God is with you and empowering you to stay on course.

"Be strong and courageous, do not be afraid or in dread of them, for the Lord your God is the One who is going with you. He will not desert you or abandon you.

Deuteronomy 31:6 NASB

One of the most common reasons why people give up on "Plan A" and start casting about for Plans B and C is that they are too impatient. They want to follow God's plan, but they want it to unfold quickly and immediately. They want it to be what I call a "microwave miracle." They'll say, "Well, I've tried to follow the Lord's plan for my life for a week now, and it doesn't seem to be working out, so I think I'll try something else."

I believe this type of thinking is a result of the world we live in. We have instant coffee, instant potatoes, and instant rice. Microwave ovens can cook in 15 minutes what used to take an hour or more. *Quicker. Faster. Immediate gratification.* Those are the buzzwords of modern America.

But it doesn't work that way in the realm of the Spirit. The manifestation of some of the things God has said to you will take time. They may require your growth and steadfast perseverance. They may involve your holding fast to His promise over a period of months or even years!

Abraham believed God's promise for a long time before he saw it come true. We all need to get to the point where we can believe and walk faithfully according to the word of the Lord, no matter how long it takes to manifest or what we see around us.

Talk to yourself if you have to: "Soul, God said this, and this *is* the way we are going to go!"

Your soul may answer you back, *Well, what about money? What about security for your family? What about a hundred other things?*

We all need to get to the point where we can believe and walk faithfully according to the word of the Lord, no matter how long it takes to manifest or what we see around us.

In the natural, these are all legitimate questions, but the word of the Lord is given a place in our lives that is higher than all of that. God's ways are higher than man's ways. His thoughts are higher than man's thoughts. His plans for us are infinitely better than the plans we could devise for ourselves (*see* Isa. 55:9; Jer. 29:11).

So don't go looking for microwave miracles. Hold fast to God's "Plan A" for your life. Walk in it and become stable in it!

WALKING IN PATIENCE

But let patience have her perfect work, that ye may be perfect and entire, wanting nothing.

James 1:4

Patience is so important — not only in the realm of the Spirit, but in the natural world as well. We can see the different results of patience versus impatience all around us.

In the world of finance, a person who saves and invests wisely and carefully will see a steady growth in their net worth. An impatient person who is always looking for a big-money, get-rich-quick scheme is always on the verge of "making it big" but never really does. This is an example of how "slow and steady" wins the race.

Consider the many quick weight-loss diets. There are some diets that can help people lose weight almost overnight. But there are a lot of discouraged people walking around who lost a lot of weight in a hurry, only to see it all come back in a very short time. It takes patience, proper eating habits, and exercise to keep your body in shape. There are no shortcuts. Patience and perseverance are the keys.

It takes patience to be a good parent. It takes patience to build a strong marriage. It takes patience to strengthen and develop your mind. And it takes patience to wait on the Lord. But these are the treasures in life that are well worth the time and spiritual fortitude required to reap the rewards.

> **But they that wait upon the Lord shall renew their strength; they shall mount up with wings as eagles; they shall run, and not be weary; and they shall walk, and not faint.**
>
> **Isaiah 40:31**

Don't think you are wasting your time by waiting before the Lord. Quite the opposite! You are gaining His strength, knowledge, and wisdom for the task ahead of you. Your patience for God's perfect timing in your life will pay off.

Now, keep in mind that patience isn't the same as inertia. I'm not talking about sitting back for months and being inactive. There is a time for patiently waiting before the Lord to listen for what He wants to say to you, and there is a time for action. And when He tells you to move, you must move!

When that time for action comes, don't be afraid. God may be calling you to do something new and different. You see, sticking with the old ways of doing something does not constitute patience. You can keep up with what God is doing in every new season and operate in patience at the same time.

> **Your patience for God's perfect timing in your life will pay off.**

One day, if the Lord tarries, the things that are occurring in the world right now will come to a divine conclusion and the Holy Spirit will begin to move the Body of Christ into what He is doing in the new season. When that happens, we will need to stay in close communion with God so we can flow with His ways and His timings, whatever that looks like. That's why it's so crucial that we are led by His Holy Spirit so we can always stay on His cutting edge — always moving forward.

God wants us to be patient and to wait upon Him, but He doesn't want us to grow fat, complacent, and lazy. His job is to lead. Our job is to follow and to hang on tenaciously to what He has said to us.

HOLDING ON TIGHT TO GOD'S WORD

When I was still a youth, God said to me, *"Go to the nations and preach. Write books, and I will sell them. Preach strong, and*

I will draw the people. Prophesy, and you will have the ability to minister to preachers."

God gave that word to me at the very beginning of my ministry, and as long as I hold fast to it and follow it, it works in my life. However, should I ever start holding to the *operation* of that word and let go of its *foundation*, it would stop working. For instance, if I ever started thinking that the books I have written are the ultimate achievement, I would stop seeing the harvest from the word of the Lord that caused them to be birthed and become successful. I have to hold fast to God's word to me and not what that word produces.

I was in high school when the Lord first told me to write books. It isn't possible to have a better literary agent than Almighty God! As long as I keep writing, trying to get the word of the Lord out to people through the printed page, I know my books will continue to sell. Although I don't have a great deal of time to devote to writing, I work at it as I'm able and it comes together just the way God told me it would.

Some people say, "I don't understand. Why does this work so well for you?" All I can say is, "I'm just following God!" It's really that simple. God told me that as I write the books He wants me to write, He would get them into the hands of those who could be blessed, encouraged, and instructed by them. My part is to simply obey Him.

**I have to hold fast to God's word to me
and not what that word produces.**

While overseas, I've had people walk up to me and hand me a copy of one of my books printed in a foreign language that I didn't even know it had been translated into! I'll have to admit, there have been times when I thought, *Now, wait a minute. Did I sign a contract authorizing this to be done?* But then I'd hear God's voice whisper to my spirit: *"I didn't say anything about a contract. I just told you to write books, and I would get them into the hands of those I want to read them."*

You see, for a brief moment I'd lose sight of what God had spoken to me. My goal and objective is that as many people as possible will read the prophetic word of God and that He will be glorified in all I do.

By the grace of God, I have more than 16 million books in print to date in more than 60 languages. Does that sound like bragging? Well, it isn't. The success of my books doesn't reflect on me personally. It reflects on what can happen when someone does what God tells him to do.

You may be facing challenges and transitions in your life. You may know beyond a shadow of a doubt that God spoke to you and revealed His plan for your life. You may have already gone through a period of time wondering, *Is this really God?* — but now you *know* it was the Lord who spoke to you.

Now is the time to hold fast to the word God gave you. Don't waver or doubt. Just yield to Him every step of the way, and allow that word to manifest in your life.

Remember the faith of Abraham. Even as he was placing Isaac on the altar, he was holding tightly to the word God had given him. He knew that even if Isaac's life was offered up as a sacrifice, God could bring the boy back from the dead in order to fulfill His word that Abraham would be the father of many nations (*see* Heb. 11:18-19).

**Now is the time to hold fast
to the word God gave you. Don't waver or doubt.
Just yield to Him every step of the way,
and allow that word to manifest in your life.**

You may be going through a drastic change in your life. Things may not have gone the way you thought they were going to go, and you don't see how they're going to change. It's easy in that kind of situation to become sad, angry, and frustrated. And in the midst of that kind of emotional mess, it can be a real temptation to let go of God's word and run back to the familiarity of yesterday and the way things used to be.

Don't do it! Hold on to God's word to you, and believe that He is able to raise your Isaac from the dead.

There have been times when the Isaac in my life was dead, and the only thing I had to hang on to was my faith in what God had said to me. When it would have been easier to say, "I quit," I had to stand and say, "I believe." I knew I couldn't quit. I had to hang on and remind myself that God is always faithful. There was nothing else to say or do. I just had to believe that God's word to me was true and that in due season, I would see the fruit that it would produce.

> **...I know whom I have believed, and am persuaded that he is able to keep that which I have committed unto him against that day.**
>
> **2 Timothy 1:12**

You can have great assurance in the knowledge that God will complete whatever work He has begun in you. He *will* finish the work if you will hold to your faith and be persuaded that He is able to perform what He said He would do.

Hold on to God's word to you, and believe that He is able to raise your Isaac from the dead.

God is able to fulfill every one of His promises in your life. He *wants* to do that for you. So hold fast to what He has told you! God is not dead but *alive*. He is almighty — *not* all-weak.

> **For I am confident of this very thing, that He who began a good work among you will complete it by the day of Christ Jesus.**
>
> **Philippians 1:6 NASB**

What is the word that the Lord has put into your heart? Don't look at your present circumstances — just find that word in your spirit and begin to pray it out. Stir it up. Keep it alive!

Pray strong on that word. Let it live again! His plans for your future are absolutely glorious! You can count on it!

CHAPTER

Receiving Remedy
and Restoration

How do you know what God is saying? How can you be sure to be in the correct timing of God? By applying the spiritual principles covered in this book, you can set your heart to hear from God and be empowered by His Spirit to do whatever He asks you to do. And you can learn to stay so in tune with His leadings that you're always where you need to be at the time you need to be there to accomplish His plan.

Let me give you a couple of key points on how to operate in God's perfect timing.

First, do not seek another person's opinion concerning what you sense in your spirit as absolute direction.

Go to the Father in prayer and say, "Father, show me the timing of these things. Make it clear to me what You desire." Once you have peace in your spirit that you have heard from the Lord, at that point it may be time to go to a trusted mentor or pastor with spiritual authority in your life to receive wise counsel — *not* someone's mere opinion — regarding the matter.

Believe the direction you receive in your spirit. What you hear in your head can often be wrong, but you will know because you won't have total peace — that peace that passes all understanding (*see* Phil. 4:7). However, when you choose to believe the direction you receive from Heaven and to follow your spirit, your obedience will always bring total peace.

Second, seek God regarding the message you hear or read from ministers of the Gospel that speaks to your spirit.

Years ago, I began to sense the anointing for warfare surfacing again in the Body of Christ, and I wrote the book, *The Invading Force.* Many people said, "Roberts sure is full of youthful zeal and fire!"

Every time I heard that, it would bother me. I knew the message was a word from God, delivered in His timing. And I knew that the attitude of those people was a sign of spiritual complacency. They were patronizing God's message instead of receiving it as from Him.

If that message was a product of youthful zeal, then I want that same kind of zeal when I am 80 years old, if the Lord tarries that long! But I heard that comment so often, I began to check myself. I went to the Lord and prayed, "God, tell me what time it is. Am I preaching what You are doing? Is this a time of war that we are coming into?"

At that time, everyone wanted to hear about love, prosperity, and other such pleasant subjects. But down in my spirit, God kept saying to me, *"The Church has come into a time of war. This is not a time of peace, but a time of spiritual conflict. You need this anointing for this time."*

When you choose to believe the direction you receive from Heaven and to follow your spirit, your obedience will always bring total peace.

Coming out of that time with the Lord, I realized that *warfare always precedes spiritual harvest.*

The best way to check the accuracy of a message or a word that resonates in your spirit is to test it according to the Bible and to pray and ask God about it. Make sure it lines up with the Word of God. Then stay with and *take heed to* the prophecies you hear in your spirit. When those things begin to be fulfilled, you will know God's timing is changing.

The world events that have transpired over the past few decades right up to this present day have shown us that we are in the last days. But even more importantly, we have seen that God will open doors in the midst of upheaval and change for the Church to reap a great harvest before the end comes.

The Lord said to me once, *"When events* [such as the Iron Curtain coming down in Eastern Europe in the early 1990s and the Russian invasion of Ukraine in recent days] *take place in the last days, they are not to be analyzed with the mind — they are to be taken advantage of. My Church needs to quit spending its time analyzing everything. Instead, it needs to recognize the door that is being opened and go through it by My Spirit!"*

**God will open doors
in the midst of upheaval and change
for the Church to reap a great harvest
before the end comes.**

Look for the doors of opportunity to preach the Gospel of the Kingdom. The fields are ripe unto harvest (*see* John 4:35)!

The Church of the last days is to be a Church that works. The Church will not have time to write books on end-time prophecy because we as believers will be too busy fulfilling those end-time prophecies! We have a duty to fulfill, not a show to watch!

For those who are staying closely tuned to Heaven, they know that God's clock is saying that revival is in progress and something is breaking open worldwide.

WHAT IF I *MISS* IT?

Suppose you miss your due season. What if, for some reason, you miss the entire timing of something God has for you? Be encouraged! God can redeem the time.

See then that ye walk circumspectly, not as fools, but as wise, redeeming the time, because the days are evil.

Ephesians 5:15-16

"Redeeming the time" means *to rescue from loss*. God can recover and redeem the time through His grace and mercy. If you miss it, get up, repent, find out what you did wrong, and go on. Don't dwell on your mistakes and throw yourself one big pity party.

What if, for some reason, you miss the entire timing of something God has for you? Be encouraged! God can redeem the time.

Use your mistakes as stepping stones, not stumbling blocks. Even if it seems there may be some things that cannot be recovered, our God is a miracle-working God. All that is required of us is that we trust Him.

How do you get to the place where God will redeem the time? Repent and tell the Lord, "Father, I'm sorry for missing it. If You arrange the time for me to do it again, I'll do it Your way. Forgive me for making the mistake. Thank You for redeeming the time for me."

You may have been middle-aged or even older when you got born again. You might not think there is much time left for you to accomplish what God has planned for your life. But you must simply make the decision, *Now I have quit running, and I agree to do what God has called me to do.* Ask the Lord to redeem the time for you so you can do more in the latter part of your life than you did in the beginning. You can be that eleventh-hour worker and share a vital role in the great, last-days harvest (*see* Matt. 20:1-16)!

I pray this book has helped you make a quality decision to pursue the price of spiritual power as you learn to more clearly discern the times. Seek God diligently about His seasons in your life, your church, your nation, and your world. I believe that you will hear from God and that as He separates the wheat and the tares in this hour, He will find you among the choice wheat in His field. You will always be at the right place at the right time, empowered and anointed to do the part God has ordained for you to fulfill in this last-days generation!

ABOUT THE AUTHOR

From a young age, Roberts Liardon was destined to become one of the most well-known Christian authors and orators of his generation. To date, he has sold more than 16 million books worldwide that have been translated into 60+ international languages to date. Roberts has ministered in 127 countries, both to the multitudes and to world leaders. He is recognized internationally and has experienced great success as a revivalist, an inspirational speaker, an author, and a Church historian.

Roberts Liardon was born in 1966 in Tulsa, Oklahoma, as the first male child born to a student of the newly launched Oral Roberts University. His career in the ministry began at the young age of 12½ when he gave his initial public address. At age 17, Liardon published his first book, *I Saw Heaven*, in which he related his experience of going to Heaven as a young boy. The book catapulted Roberts into the public eye and sold more than 1.5 million copies. Over the next few years, he became one of the leading public speakers in the Christian community all over the world.

When Roberts was 12½ years old, Jesus appeared to him in a vision and told him to study the great preachers — to learn both of their successes and failures. From that day on, Roberts began to devote himself to this study. This lifelong pursuit has established him as a leading Protestant Church historian, a role he carries with honor to this day.

The day came when God spoke further to Roberts about writing and producing both a DVD series and a book series entitled "God's Generals." The original mission was to chronicle the lives of some of the leading Pentecostal and Charismatic leaders so the Body could learn from both their successes and failures. The DVD series was an immediate success, becoming one of the best-selling Christian DVD series in the history of Christian media. The "God's Generals" book series is an ongoing assignment that also found a worldwide reading audience that has continued to grow over the years.

In 1990, Roberts Liardon moved to Southern California and founded his worldwide headquarters in Orange County. There he and his team founded Embassy Christian Center and Spirit Life Bible College, both of which became among the largest and most influential in the region.

In 2007, Roberts moved his ministry headquarters to Sarasota, Florida, where it is currently located. In 2009, he accepted the position as principal of the International Bible Institute of London, the training arm of the Kensington London City Church. It was a position he held for five years as an assignment from God to help further His plans and purposes for the United Kingdom and Europe.

Roberts Liardon continues to speak to this generation in pulpits across the United States and around the world. He also produces his own online courses, where he teaches on God's Generals and other key Bible truths necessary to strengthen the Body of Christ for this critical hour we live in.

Throughout the years, Liardon has continued to be a significant contributor toward building God's Kingdom, with the belief that relationships are the key element that bonds the staff at Roberts Liardon Ministries to people around the world. Each year millions are touched through this worldwide ministry, a genuine resource of victory for the entire Body of Christ.

CONTACT

ROBERTS LIARDON MINISTRIES

For further information
about Roberts Liardon Ministries,
please visit the ministry website at
www.robertsliardon.org

or write us at:

U.S. Office:
Roberts Liardon Ministries
P.O. Box 4215
Sarasota, FL 34230
941-748-3883
Email: info@robertsliardon.org

Canada Office:
Roberts Liardon Ministries Canada
2A-13139 80 Ave.
Surrey BC V3W 3B1
604-594-7327
Email: info@robertsliardon.org

UK/Europe Office:
Roberts Liardon Ministries UK/Europe
22 Notting Hill Gate, Suite 125
London WII 3JE, England
Email: info@robertsliardon.org

Other ways to connect:

Facebook: Roberts Liardon Official
Twitter: @RobertsLiardon
Instagram: @robertsliardon_official
YouTube: Roberts Liardon

The *Supernatural* Language

Why You Should Speak in Tongues
by Dr. Roberts Liardon

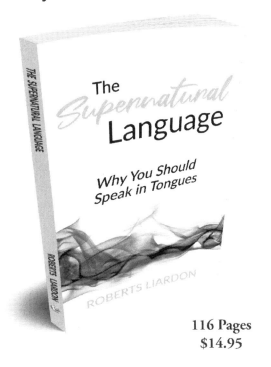

116 Pages
$14.95

In his book *The Supernatural Language*, Roberts Liardon brings clarity to the basics you must know to be filled with the Holy Spirit and receive the supernatural language He wants to give you. Then Roberts takes you across the threshold to give you glimpses into the exciting journey that lies just ahead of you once you are fully and supernaturally equipped from the inside out!

To order, please visit our online store at:
www.robertsliardon.org, or call the RLM office at:
941-748-3883